Biblical Principles for Successful Living

Discovering Your Purpose and the Tools to Accomplish It

WILLIAM LAKE

Copyright © 2019 William Lake.

All rights reserved. No part of this book may be used or reproduced by any means, graphic, electronic, or mechanical, including photocopying, recording, taping or by any information storage retrieval system without the written permission of the author except in the case of brief quotations embodied in critical articles and reviews.

This book is a work of non-fiction. Unless otherwise noted, the author and the publisher make no explicit guarantees as to the accuracy of the information contained in this book and in some cases, names of people and places have been altered to protect their privacy.

WestBow Press books may be ordered through booksellers or by contacting:

WestBow Press
A Division of Thomas Nelson & Zondervan
1663 Liberty Drive
Bloomington, IN 47403
www.westbowpress.com
1 (866) 928-1240

Because of the dynamic nature of the Internet, any web addresses or links contained in this book may have changed since publication and may no longer be valid. The views expressed in this work are solely those of the author and do not necessarily reflect the views of the publisher, and the publisher hereby disclaims any responsibility for them.

Any people depicted in stock imagery provided by Getty Images are models, and such images are being used for illustrative purposes only.
Certain stock imagery © Getty Images.

Scripture taken from the New King James Version®. Copyright © 1982 by Thomas Nelson. Used by permission. All rights reserved.

Scripture quotations marked (NIV) are taken from the Holy Bible, New International Version®, NIV®. Copyright © 1973, 1978, 1984, 2011 by Biblica, Inc.™ Used by permission of Zondervan. All rights reserved worldwide. www.zondervan.com The "NIV" and "New International Version" are trademarks registered in the United States Patent and Trademark Office by Biblica, Inc.™

Scripture quotations taken from the Amplified® Bible (AMP),
Copyright © 2015 by The Lockman Foundation
Used by permission. www.Lockman.org

ISBN: 978-1-9736-4996-0 (sc)
ISBN: 978-1-9736-4997-7 (hc)
ISBN: 978-1-9736-4995-3 (e)

Library of Congress Control Number: 2018915116

Print information available on the last page.

WestBow Press rev. date: 1/9/2019

Note to the Reader

I began writing this book in 2011 and have taken far too long to complete it. Since that time, I have observed that there are many books and sermons covering some of these ideas. My original purpose was simply to write something, print some copies, and provide these copies to the kids before they went off to college, which I did. Then I continued to improve upon it.

At one point I received an advertisement about self-publishing a book. It seemed like a good idea, and I decided to do it. In turn I would receive copies of the book that I could give away as well as various author support functions. I imagine some of these will be sold as well by the publisher, though that is not part of my motivation for this effort.

The purpose of this somewhat comprehensive self-published book is to help people — in particular young people — develop a strong faith in God, discern a life purpose early, and employ Judeo-Christian biblical principles throughout their lives to realize their God-given destinies. One of my sons is a youth pastor, and my hope is that he can refer to this from time to time for lesson preparation.

The book is an accumulation of wisdom I have gathered throughout my life to date. All of the principles described in this book are now part of my world outlook and my life philosophy. I learned some of these ideas the hard way from experience, and most from other Christians and/or experts over my lifetime of reading, watching Christian television, hearing sermons, and attending church and Bible studies.

It is not my intention to indicate or imply that every idea, or even most of the ideas in this book, originated with me. I seek to collect and uniquely present these adopted or self-developed ideas to help young people grow in Christ and in their understanding of biblical applications for successful kingdom living. Where an idea is uniquely attributable to one particular source that I remember, I happily note it. Whenever possible, I explicitly mention or note the source of the ideas in this book entering my life.

It is my particular hope that this book will become useful to church youth groups. All is to the glory of God and the building of His kingdom.

The Vision

Every significant endeavor should have a clear, concise, compelling vision statement — easy to understand, clarifying in purpose, and stimulating in understanding and action. It is appropriate to make such a vision statement for this book.

That people will know, love, and honor the true God and discover their life's purpose; excel in life and expand God's Kingdom, utilizing biblical principles; become persons of influence, changing the world through Christian love in action.

Acknowledgements

I would like to thank my dear wife, Melanie, who is very spiritual and creative, and is a wonderful partner in serving the Lord, for providing the encouragement to "just keep going" and finish this book.

I would like to acknowledge the contribution of our friend Jane Holley. We met Jane while volunteering at a local food bank, and she was kind enough to offer her editorial services. Jane made several very helpful additions, deletions, and suggestions toward making the manuscript better. I am indebted to her expertise and willingness to participate in this project. The book is better because of Jane.

I would also like to thank Dr. Joshua Davis for reading the manuscript and making many helpful suggestions. Thank you, Josh, for your suggestions regarding syntax, organization, and elaboration.

I would like to thank Pastor Christian Lake for his insights and useful suggestions toward making the manuscript more engaging and appealing to the reader.

As the project neared completion, the publisher suggested some areas for improvement. I enlisted the help of Jim Hastings of Huntsville, AL, who is a skilled author and editor. Jim did a great job editing and commenting, and I now believe this book is as good as it can be and is ready to go forward.

I am profoundly grateful for my mom and dad, who are the best parents anyone could ever want. I am particularly appreciative of the helpful suggestions of my mother, Tina Golden.

Finally, I want to thank our kids — Christian, Jordan, Joshua, Megan, Mark, Damonne, and Charlotte. You have made us so proud of you and what you have become. You all are a constant source of joy to us. Use your time wisely on this earth, and you will reap eternal blessings.

Only what you do for Christ will last.

Dedication

This book is dedicated to God our Father, who includes in His family all who believe in the name of His Son, Jesus. To Jesus, our Savior, who gave His life so that we can live with God forever. And to the Holy Spirit, our Counselor who abides in us, giving us revelation of the Word of God unto salvation, wisdom, and victory in life.

Contents

Introduction xv

Chapter 1	The Most Important Thing I Can Tell You 1
Chapter 2	Quick and Simple Bible Overview to Start 5
Chapter 3	The Recipe for a Successful Life in a Nutshell 11
Chapter 4	Does God Really Exist? And if So, Is There Really Only One God? 15
Chapter 5	What's Your Purpose for Being Here? 27
Chapter 6	You Are Thinking Your Future Now! 35
Chapter 7	How Your Words Help You Achieve Your Goals 51
Chapter 8	Your Choices Show Who and What You Will Become . . . 59
Chapter 9	A Few Random Pieces of Advice 69
Chapter 10	How to Get Closer to God 79
Chapter 11	The Most Important Concept Expanded Upon 87
Chapter 12	Why Feelings and Fears Must Not Be Your Guides 99
Chapter 13	Things to Know About Marriage and Relationships 107
Chapter 14	Are Grace and Mercy That Big of a Deal? 117
Chapter 15	Some Tips for Succeeding in College or Trade School . . . 123
Chapter 16	Are Miracles and Healings Still Happening Today? 131
Chapter 17	What's Coming Next for This World and Us? 139
Chapter 18	Develop Amnesia When Necessary! 145
Chapter 19	Satan's Dilemma — Then and Now 149
Chapter 20	Stay on the Path 151
Chapter 21	Some Scriptures to Think Harder About 155
Chapter 22	We Want to Meet the Lord and Hear "Well Done" 161
Chapter 23	The Most Important Day of My Life 165
Chapter 24	Go with God 167

Introduction

In developing some of these ideas, I will occasionally mention fictitious characters called John and Jim. Their experiences help illustrate several of the major points. Any resemblance to actual persons, living or dead, is purely coincidental.

Also, if appropriate, I have used **bold type** or *italics* to highlight important ideas in a chapter.

In this book I frequently use the term Satan. Christian doctrine tells us that Satan can only be in one place at a time, so he cannot be personally influencing everyone all the time. The term Satan in this book refers to demonic or evil forces under satanic control that may affect Christians directly or indirectly, principally through thoughts and ideas and all the influences currently embedded in our world. Satan is our enemy — the enemy of our souls. But he is not God's equal.

Chapter 1
The Most Important Thing I Can Tell You

While experiencing life with other people, hearing countless sermons, and reading many books, I realized that there is one major piece of advice that is most helpful to the Christian. It is one simple action point: *Just keep going.*

The life of a Christian is just as challenging, if not more so, than that of the non-Christian. We are not promised an easy life because we are believers. Sometimes the road ahead can seem very long and the destination unclear. Sometimes the negative events of life can discourage us. Sometimes our own minds become our worst enemies. I have experienced many difficult circumstances and have witnessed many of my friends — as well as people I know and many in the news — experience horrible circumstances.

We are all no doubt protected from many things each day by a mighty, merciful, patient God. But occasionally things that are not desirable do happen. Sometimes even terrible or life-changing events occur. We should pray vigorously against these eventualities with faith before they even happen, but life does happen sooner or later. If nothing else, some of those we love will die at some point in our lifetimes. When you or a loved one is very sick or someone you care deeply about dies, you have to just keep going.

You may have failed miserably, lost a job, or are having financial problems. Just keep going. If you have been wrongly accused or slandered, just keep going. If you dream of achieving something great and your plans, year after year, don't come to fruition — and if your opinions and efforts are neither sought nor appreciated — just keep going.

When fear grips your heart and mind as terror strikes in the world and you fear for your country, your family, the future of your finances, your health, or your kids, put your trust in God and just keep going. When it seems that you are pedaling and pedaling but going nowhere and that God has left you on a shelf somewhere, just keep going. He is always there, whether you see and feel Him or not. He is always at work around us and within us.

When you reach a ripe old age and are still confronted with the painful fact that you have much more to learn, that you need to improve in a variety of areas, or that you make the same mistakes over and over, just keep going. When relentlessly confronted with guilt and shame for the mistakes of your past and pounded with the defamations of the evil one, saying that you are not worthy to serve the Lord or to be with Him forever, learn to believe right and just keep going.

And while you keep going, take time to consider each life situation you are presented with in order to learn from it. Be sure to thank God for getting involved in your life and, in many cases, molding you into His image through these events. Each situation holds its own life lessons. Each situation confronts you with opportunities to look into the mirror and see who you really are and what you need to improve.

If you feel the whole world is wrong and you are right, and that you have simply once again become a victim of all the evil people or circumstances in the world, beware. Learn what you can from each situation in the areas of self-improvement and the development of biblical character, and keep going.

As you go through this book and learn to routinely employ its principles for a more meaningful life, never forget this exhortation: Tough times will come. Pain and suffering will come. Disappointments will come. Expect them, and keep on going. Don't be overcome by the discouragement and disappointment of unmet expectations. Never quit learning, growing, and loving.

Through life's circumstances, God teaches us what we need to know to become equipped for His effective service in this life and the next one. Life's circumstances, seen through the lens of the immutable Word of God, are our tutors. They lead us into revealing introspection, personal growth, and usefulness to the Kingdom of God, now and forever. Let

Biblical Principles for Successful Living

your overriding goal be to become more Christlike, and you will never be a failure — no matter the event or outcome.

Chapter 2
Quick and Simple Bible Overview to Start

The purpose of this chapter is to help you understand the Bible. The Bible is full of rich stories and themes that we can enjoy and learn principles from for all eternity — without exhausting the wisdom therein. You can spend your whole life memorizing, studying, and learning from the Bible.

This chapter gives you a simple Bible overview of how it all fits together so that the Scriptures will not be frightening or intimidating. The Bible is the story of God and His chosen people, Israel, who were to bring the message of God's love to all the world, to include the revelation of Messiah.

The book of Genesis tells how it all began. The story starts out with God creating the heavens and the earth and finally man. Adam and Eve were created to be God's representatives on earth. The vast majority of Bible (human) time passes in Genesis. Adam and Eve allowed sin to enter the world by their disobedience and yielded their (our) God-given dominion over the earth to Satan, who immediately sought to ruin humankind. Seeing the proliferation of evil, God destroyed most of humankind in the flood.

Noah and his family were the only righteous ones left on earth. As a result of taking shelter in the Ark, Noah and his three sons — Shem, Ham, and Japheth — and their families survived to repopulate the earth. All three sons had families, but through the line of Shem came a very important person: Abraham. Abraham was chosen by God and received God's promise that God would bless him and his descendants — and that they would be as numerous as the stars in the sky. Abraham begat Isaac, and Isaac begat Jacob.

Jacob had twelve sons. These would initially become the twelve tribes of Israel. The people of God, the Israelites, grew in number and expanded in influence. These were, and are, God's chosen people: the Hebrews (not called Jews until later). Abraham was told that his descendants would be captive in a foreign land for four hundred years.

One of Jacob's twelve sons was named Joseph. His mistreatment by his brothers resulted in his slavery and imprisonment in Egypt. However, Joseph's eventual elevation to second in command by Pharaoh, after he had interpreted Pharaoh's dreams, caused all the Hebrew people in Jacob's family, around seventy-five, to eventually go to Egypt. There, during a great famine, they were fed and protected by Pharaoh and Joseph in the beautiful land of Goshen. God's chosen people went to live in the land of Egypt, thanks to Joseph's divinely orchestrated position under Pharaoh.

The eventual leadership in Egypt forgot the Joseph story. They required that the Hebrew people become their slaves and treated them badly. The Hebrews cried out to God for a deliverer. God would choose Moses. After four hundred years, it was time for them to leave Egypt and go to the land that God planned for them to dwell in. This was the land of Canaan and was called the Promised Land. Initially led by God's prophet Moses, more than two million Hebrews left Egypt to head to the Promised Land.

During the journey from Egypt, which should have taken a few weeks but ended up taking forty years, the Lord taught His people His standards and His plan for them. This is what the first five books of the Bible are about. They are called the *Torah,* or God's Holy Law. In the first five books of the Bible, God teaches His children how He wants them to live — with many examples and trials in the desert. God was present with them in the desert via the tabernacle, which was His temporary dwelling on earth.

Moses disobeyed God at one point and was prevented from actually entering the Promised Land. After Moses died, Joshua became the leader of the Israelites. The book of Joshua tells us about this.

The Hebrews eventually entered their land with Joshua as their leader and began to take possession of it by force as directed. They did not fully eliminate other inhabitants from the land, however, and these inhabitants occasionally came back to trouble them. After Joshua died, the people began to do evil things, such as worshipping false gods, intermarrying with the people of the lands, and consulting false prophets. As a result, they were overrun by enemies. When they were tormented by their enemies, they cried out to God for help. God raised up people to deliver them from the hands of their enemies. These people were called the judges.

The judges were successful in getting the Hebrews, who were sinful in their behavior, back in line with God. In each case, things would go well for a while, but then Israel would act badly and become oppressed by another enemy. Then the people would cry for help, and God would raise up another judge to defeat the enemy causing the problem. Things would go well for a while and the people's behavior would deteriorate again, and then things would go badly again for the Israelites. This is where stories of famous judges from the book of Judges, such as Gideon, Samson, Deborah, Jephthah, and others, are found.

The people of Israel eventually asked the last judge, the prophet Samuel, for a king. God warned them that they should not do so. They insisted, however, and King Saul was selected. King Saul did not obey God completely. He angered God because of his incomplete obedience and was eventually replaced as king of God's people by David, a man after God's own heart. David was the leader God told to establish Jerusalem as the place where God would put His name.

David's son Solomon was established as king over Israel after David died. Solomon is said to be the wisest and richest man who ever lived. He built the first great temple in Jerusalem, which replaced the temporary tabernacle. Even though he was the wisest man on the Earth, he followed after some of the gods of his many foreign wives, and he angered God. This is all outlined in the books of First and Second Samuel, First and Second Kings, First and Second Chronicles, and Ecclesiastes. Some of the angst of Solomon and the wisdom he gained from a complicated life appears in Proverbs and Ecclesiastes.

As a result of Solomon's incomplete obedience by following after other gods with his foreign wives, the unified kingdom of Israel was split into a northern and a southern kingdom after Solomon's death. The northern kingdom, Israel, consisted of ten tribes and had nineteen kings, none of whom obeyed God. The southern kingdom consisted principally of two tribes, Judah and Benjamin, and was called Judah or Jerusalem (enter the terms *Jews* and *Jewish*). It had twenty kings, many of whom were good kings who obeyed the Lord. Among the kings of Judah, eight were considered good by most — Asa, Jehoshaphat, Joash, Amaziah, Azariah, Jotham, Hezekiah, and Josiah. This is also outlined in the 12 books of history such as First and Second Samuel, First and Second Kings, and First and Second Chronicles. These books are all about the history of the two kingdoms and all of their kings.

While many of the kings of the southern kingdom, Judah, were obedient kings who honored God, both kingdoms had periods of worshipping foreign gods and doing things that displeased God. This is where the prophets come in. The five books of the major prophets — Isaiah, Jeremiah, Lamentations, Ezekiel, and Daniel — as well as the twelve books of the minor prophets — including Joel, Amos, Hosea, Nahum, Jonah, Obadiah, and Habakkuk — talk about the events of these days and give many warnings to the people to repent and follow God. These are the books that detail the warnings of God through His prophets to the two kingdoms and many other surrounding nations. The prophets prophesied to the northern and southern kingdoms, as well as many of the surrounding kingdoms that mistreated Israel, that they should repent and follow after God. The prophets spoke to the kingdoms and their kings about the current and future ramifications of their choices.

Most of the prophetic books have several components to them, such as a past (remember what God did for us); a present (look at what you are doing now, and here is what God says about it); a near future (this is what is going to happen in the immediate future if you do not stop doing what you are doing); and a far future (the Messiah is coming, and all will be right again when you are dwelling in your land after you have been dispersed and you return and your enemies are destroyed). Many prophecies of Jesus as Messiah can be found in the books of the prophets.

Ultimately, neither kingdom obeyed God fully. First, the northern kingdom fell to the invading army from Assyria and was carried away around 720 BC. The Assyrians filled the land with people of other lands who mingled with the remnant of Israel. This is where the term Samaritan comes from, and is why Jews and Samaritans were at odds with each other. The southern kingdom lasted until around 586 BC as an independent kingdom because it had many good kings, but eventually it fell to the invading army of King Nebuchadnezzar from Babylon. In that invasion, the first temple, which was built by Solomon, was destroyed. The southern kingdom then spent seventy years in captivity (exile) in Babylon before returning.

Some of the prophets plied their God-given trade during the exile in Babylon and after the return to Israel. Eventually, Israel was allowed to go back to Jerusalem by Cyrus, King of Persia, after Babylon was defeated by the Medo-Persians. This is where Ezra, Esther, Nehemiah, and other books describe events such as the returning, the rebuilding of the city, the rebuilding of the wall, and the re-building of the second temple at Jerusalem. Other Old Testament books include the five books of poetry and wisdom — Job, Psalms, Proverbs, Ecclesiastes, and the Song of Solomon.

The last Old Testament prophet is Malachi, who spoke after the kingdom of Judah was back in the land of Israel. Then there was a silence in the land during which God did not speak through His prophets. After about 400 years, the Messiah Yeshua (Jesus) came as prophesied. However, He was not recognized by most of the people, since He was not a conquering king at the time; and He was crucified, killed, and buried. He was raised again on the third day, just as had been prophesied.

Jesus' ministry was to the Jewish people primarily, and this is all outlined in the four Gospels. Jesus kept His Father's law (the Torah) and, as the prophets foretold, He showed us how to obey God with a heart of love, being led by the Spirit (see Deuteronomy 18). He tells us that salvation and access to God will be only through Him by grace through faith. We must believe on Him.

After Jesus died, rose from the dead, and went to heaven, He revealed Himself on the road to Damascus to the great Pharisee Saul of Tarsus, better known to us as St. Paul, who would become a major evangelist and apostle. The Lord told him to take the gospel of grace to the Gentiles. Paul's journeys are detailed in the book of Acts, which tells of Paul's and a few of the other apostles' travels, speaking and preaching the gospel of Jesus Christ to Jews and Gentiles around the known world.

When Jesus revealed Himself to Paul and told him to share the gospel with the Gentiles, the age of the Gentiles, or the Church Age, began. The

Church Age, during which all people are allowed to join God's family by faith in Christ, continues to this day. We are essentially grafted in to the Jewish chosen people by God's mercy. All people — Jews and Gentiles — can now join God's family — but only through faith in Christ.

Much Christian theology, encouragement, and warnings to avoid false teaching are found in the epistles written by Paul, such as Galatians, Ephesians, Romans, Titus, First and Second Timothy, and others. There are also epistles written by John, James, Peter, and Jude. All of these books tell us about Jesus and instruct us regarding how we should live as Christians. All of these books stress God's loving provision of Christ as our Savior and the importance of obedience to Him. Most also stress the importance of living by faith and love rather than putting our trust in our own good works by keeping the Law.

The book of Hebrews is a fantastic book whose authorship is uncertain but was probably written by Paul. It compares and contrasts the Law given by Moses with the salvation by grace through faith in Jesus Christ. The final sacrifice for sin and the fulfillment of God's righteous requirements are due to Christ's death and resurrection and are held in contrast to the repeated animal sacrifices in the temple, which were only shadow pictures of the perfect lamb (Christ) who was to come.

Eventually, and likely fairly soon, the time of the Gentiles will come to an end, and Israel will take center stage again. Never make the mistake of assuming God is done with the Jewish people and that Christians are now the only ones who matter to God. This mistaken teaching is also known as replacement theology. The destiny of God's precious chosen people is most clearly chronicled in the books of Daniel and Revelation, as well as in the writings of many of the prophets such as Zechariah. The end times and the future establishment of the Kingdom of God for one thousand years, as well as the New Heaven and the New Earth, are all outlined in Revelation.

Enjoy the wonderful book, the Bible, on a lifetime adventure of discovery through its 39 Old Testament books and 27 New Testament books, most of which lead us directly or indirectly to God through Jesus the Messiah. Feel free to do an Internet search for a great Bible outline. You will be amazed at how it ties together. As we often hear these days, "You can't make this stuff up."

Chapter 3
The Recipe for a Successful Life in a Nutshell

Proverbs 1:7: "The fear of the LORD is the beginning of knowledge, but fools despise wisdom and instruction."

Employing good principles, just like having faith in God, has no downside. If you learn and employ them, you will substantially increase your probability of a meaningful life.

What is the main message in this book? It is as follows: Evaluate and come to the firm conclusion that there is a God and then decide who exactly God is and what He requires of you. Next, find your life's purpose and employ the techniques that will help you achieve it while helping others along the way. Never quit in your quest to gain wisdom, to contribute to society, to become more Christlike, and to positively influence your world.

It is very difficult to write a *how to* book about something as comprehensive as living a meaningful and fully successful life. There have been many books written on self-help subjects, attempting to tell us the secret formulas for accomplishing our dreams. Americans spend a great deal on self-improvement, as we can see from the many books, magazines, and speakers focused on this area. My experience is that most people don't change for the better or see significant results despite their studies and expenditures in the area of self-improvement. **The secret to realizing self-improvement is putting what you read and learn from others into action. Acting on what you learn from books and mentors is the key to success. Pick one thing at a time to improve.**

The same is true for spiritual matters. Christians may think that in spiritual matters, desired results will drop into their laps because they have good intentions and they pray. Typically, a Christian will want to know God better, experience Him, and live a more godly life. But Christians must actively participate in their personal growth and exert strenuous efforts to bring about desired results. God must be our first priority. Why wouldn't He be? Everyone knows that eternity is a very long time. Determining how we will spend it should be first on our *to do* list. So, we must get to know who God is and what He expects of us.

Controlling the mind and the thought life should be the next priority. The mind is a powerful tool, and from its proper focus, we can obtain positive results. We should manage our minds, just as we would any other part of the body. Everything begins with a thought. Be careful of the thoughts and ideas you adopt and entertain. Ideas drive behaviors. Behaviors become habits which create your future. Much of our quality of life springs from the condition of our minds. What is going on between our ears frames our entire world. You will become what you believe you can become within the bounds of Scripture and your God-given capabilities.

Actions and habits spring from thoughts and words. Words are powerful and should not be wasted or carelessly offered. Don't just babble. Use your words to help yourself and others achieve desired results. They should encourage and inspire you and those with whom you associate. You can really make someone's day with words of sincere praise.

Make your actions count. Continually sow good seed with your actions to get good results. The natural law of sowing seeds and reaping a specific harvest is also true in the practical and spiritual arenas. If you sow exercise and eat right, you will reap fitness. If you sow study time, you will reap knowledge and good grades. If you sow to the Spirit by seeking the Lord, you will reap from the Spirit a more rewarding spiritual experience and a closer walk with God. If you sow to the flesh or the carnal nature by enjoying certain of the world's many pleasures, you will find yourself becoming slave to insatiable masters that will negatively influence many of your choices. Sow good action seed to get good results. Wrong thoughts yield wrong words, wrong actions, and bad consequences; while good thoughts, words, and actions generally yield good consequences.

Biblical Principles for Successful Living

Accept the fact that what you think, say, and do will impact your future — and adjust accordingly. If we would put everything we think, say, and do to that simple test, we would make wiser choices, live better lives, and move faster toward our desired destinations. There should be no more speaking, thinking, or doing things that do not get us closer to our goals. Work, think, and speak to bring about the outcomes you truly desire. Manage your thoughts, words, and actions each day, just as you would tend to the plants in a garden.

Life is all about choices. Your future is the result of your daily choices. The secret to successfully overcoming in life is making one good choice at a time — living well from one moment to the next. Life can be lived, battles can be won, and success can be had, but only one moment at a time. The past is gone forever, and the future may not come; but we have the present that we can work with by the grace of God. Habits form over time, one action at a time. Good thoughts, good words, good deeds, and good habits will yield good results.

Be your own biggest supporter. Be your own best friend. In this life, you will have many detractors — those who will seek to diminish your achievements and potential. Don't let them do so. Do not cooperate with them. Do not agree with things that are not helpful to you and that do not encourage you to excel. Believe what God says about you rather than what other people say about you.

This book is aimed primarily at young people forming their personalities and habits, but can be helpful for people of any age seeking a change for the better through the application of better principles and more productive practices.

The principles in this book will help you find and achieve your life's purpose.

A young man — let's call him John — was raised in a mainstream denomination that offered standard religious fare. He grew up believing the typical religious "do good and God loves me; do bad and God is angry with me" theology. John believed that God was in the heavens, carefully and critically watching his every move. John's parents occasionally attended church and never had much to say in the home about the true gospel of grace or successful Christian living. John struggled with all of the issues that young men struggle with. His parents, not biblically literate, had no theological basis from which to help him make good moral choices or to develop a relationship with God.

John also grew up believing that the universe and the world came into being through the process of evolution, as he had learned in school, and that the Bible was not a book to be understood literally or utilized in daily life. If the creation story is not valid, he reckoned, how can any part of the Bible be used as a guide to live by? John made his moral decisions by doing what seemed right to most people — or asking his friends. Once he asked a church leader a question about dating. The leader erroneously informed him it was a good idea for him to be sexually active with his girlfriend because it would teach him how to become a good husband. John was pretty much on his own spiritually. His parents eventually divorced, and his father married again. John grew up believing that marriage could and should be terminated if one partner was not "happy."

One Sunday John attended a different church with a friend. After the sermon, the pastor gave an "altar call," in which he asked if anyone would like to "receive Jesus as his or her personal Savior" and gain the assurance of heaven in the afterlife. Not knowing exactly what that meant, but knowing deep inside that he needed God, John raised his hand, went forward to the altar for prayer, and said he wanted to receive Jesus as his Savior. He left church that day feeling "on top of the world," entering what some Christians call the "honeymoon phase." He felt that he was walking on air — with the joy of knowing that he belonged to Almighty God and that he would not go to hell.

Yet, after that time, John sought biblical truth only occasionally, seeking wisdom on how to live. He was never "discipled," however, and over time, many doubts and questions came to his mind that remained unresolved. He never formed a solid theological base and began to wonder if he would really go to heaven when he died, since he still occasionally sinned, and almost always was tempted to sin. John constantly confessed his sin and was always focused on "staying right with God." He wondered if he was really "saved," given this kind of erratic behavior. Honestly, he wondered who God really was, how he should live, what the spiritual life was all about, and if he could be certain of a heavenly reward.

Chapter 4

Does God Really Exist? And if So, Is There Really Only One God?

Matthew 6:33: "But seek first the kingdom of God and His righteousness, and all these things shall be added to you."

Even though John prayed the "prayer of salvation," asking Jesus to be his Savior, he sometimes wondered if there really was only one God; and if there was only one God, who exactly was He? Was Christianity the only way to God, or were there other religions as well that would yield eternal life? John wanted to know if the Bible could really tell him how to live each day. He wondered if the Old Testament was still useful or if it was just the New Testament that he should exclusively read and follow. And, of course, he wondered which parts of the Bible were true, since everyone "knew" that evolution created life and the universe. He struggled with the creation story and the authority of Scripture in general.

There are so many beliefs in the world, he thought to himself. Is it possible that God would limit Himself to only one of these belief systems? Wouldn't He accept everyone? He wondered if all the billions of people in the world would go to heaven, no matter what they believed — except, of course, the really bad ones! Are there any absolute standards, or should everyone do what seems right to them?

John had many unanswered questions deep inside — such as "Why do bad things happen to good people?" He went about his business each day, not really knowing how to answer these questions for himself or others. Even though he proclaimed himself a Christian, John quietly accepted the idea that God must be uninvolved, since there was so much pain in the world, and universally accepting because so many people believed so many things. He reasoned that maybe it did not really matter what he believed and that he should just try to be a good person. After all, how could just one concept of God be correct?

The most important question in life should be asked and answered first. The most important decision — the one about what and who to believe in — must be made first. Eternity is a very long time. As with any major undertaking, the upfront decisions count the most and set the stage for what follows. A person's spiritual life and eternal destiny are certainly no different. Some people obviously feel a keen awareness of and a strong need to know their creator. They have always felt an urgent and compelling need to resolve who God is and what they need to do to know Him. But what about everyone else? Are they curious about God as well?

The famous scientist Blaise Paschal is widely known to have said words to the effect that there is a great void inside all people that can only be filled by God. In fact, many of our greatest scientific minds were devoutly religious and believed in God and the Bible.[1] In the book of Romans, Chapter 1, Paul says that all men can see the evidence of God in nature and in everything around them, even if they have no religious training — so no one has an excuse for ignoring the existence of God. Then, according to Paul — and Paschal — we all sense the existence of God in creation, and we all have the obligation to know our Creator and resolve our eternal purpose and destinies.

To make a good decision about eternity, we need good information. An atheist does not know enough to definitively say there is no God; he or she can only be an agnostic, which means "one without knowledge" — an "ignoramus" according to the Latin translation. To authoritatively deny the existence of God, one would need complete knowledge of all things. Such a person would need to have traveled to the far corners of this universe — and any others! — searching God out, presumably coming up empty.

Humankind's knowledge of the world and the universe, even now, is severely limited. At this late date in human scientific development, the fact is, we know very little about the universe. Our knowledge of

---

[1] Evidence for God. http://www.godandscience.org/apologetics/sciencefaith.html.

biology — and, in fact, our knowledge of everything — is very limited compared to all the information that could be known. While impressive and growing, when compared to a knowledge that could fully explain phenomena such as the body and DNA, or the workings of the universe, our accumulated wisdom is meager. How can anyone dogmatically assert that there is no God or creator? Worse yet, how can anyone teach young people in schools that there is no creator, given the possible behavioral, moral, and spiritual ramifications of such a belief?

The argument for evolution is very weak. In my opinion, believing in evolution takes greater faith than believing in creation or intelligent design. If a person were walking in the forest and found a bottle cap on the ground, then he or she would be certain that it was created by an intelligent designer, not that it simply evolved there. Yet, the atheistic evolutionist says that the universe, the stars, all chemicals, and human beings, in all their complexity and creativity, simply evolved from virtually nothing to ever more complex configurations. They insist that there was no intelligent designer. Some believe in evolution with God involved — theistic evolution — which is a slightly different case, but equally difficult to support, except in the case of variation within a species, which is loosely termed evolution as well.

When one considers the myriad precisely arranged proteins in even the simplest cellular structures, they will realize that the probabilities of evolution forming such strands by chance are considered mathematically impossible. DNA contains information and actually creates life. It is itself "intelligent." It is essentially a detailed instruction book that actually writes itself as I once heard Ray Comfort point out in one of his films. Many sources indicate that it is virtually impossible for life to have evolved by chance, given the complexity of cellular activity, proteins, DNA, and RNA — as well as other structures such as the brain.[2]

Charles Darwin was one of the most severe critics of his own theory. Despite all the fossils found, there is not a single clearly transitional species proving a causal relationship between any two species.[3] There is

---

[2] Evolution Cruncher, Chapter 8. DNA and Protein. http://www.godrules.net/evolutioncruncher/c08.htm.

[3] Fossils Show Stasis and No Transitional Forms. The Institute For Creation Research, ICR.org. www.icr.org/fossils-stasis.

an abundance of micro-evolution or what is better termed as "variation" *within* a species or kind, which is supported by the biblical text; but no macro-evolution or transition between species exists.

There are also excellent arguments disputing the validity of several if not all evolutionary "pillars." For example, carbon-dating is not scientifically compelling in all cases — for several reasons, not the least of which is the relatively short half-life of Carbon 14, rendering amounts of it imperceptible after, for example, millions of years. The theoretical "geological column" shows earth layers with their alleged ages. It depends upon circular reasoning, often dating each layer with associated fossils and the same fossils by their associated layers.

There are many other dubious arguments presented to support evolution. I would like to give credit to Dr. Kent Hovind for sharing some of these ideas I just mentioned. I recommend his books and DVDs or his Creation Seminar on YouTube.[4]

Consider the universe for a moment. The fact that the earth is nicely situated in the solar system, which is perfectly placed in the galaxy at just the right location to support life, is amazing. Perfect conditions exist to support life on our planet. The earth is marvelously designed. The amount of water on earth has neither been added to nor subtracted from since its creation; the atmosphere holds the right gases in the right amounts; and the soil has the nutrients to grow the food we need. Plants, animals, and resources replenish as needed. And if the earth were positioned differently in the solar system or the galaxy, none of this would be possible. For a more complete discussion of these ideas, I recommend the works of Dr. Hugh Ross, in particular his books *The Creator and the Cosmos* and *The Fingerprint of God*.[5]

Intelligent design or creation really seems to be obvious. Therefore, a more interesting question than "Is there a creator?" might be "Who is the creator?" There are certainly many faiths and gods to believe in. Don't be too lazy to do this analysis for yourself if you have doubts. The stakes are very high. Take time to become convinced of your beliefs. Being convinced of your beliefs will help you when people challenge them.

---

[4] Kent Hovind Official. https://www.youtube.com/channel/UCxiEtqPja47nnqsJNrdOIQQ.
[5] Hugh Ross, *The Creator and the Cosmos* (Covina, CA: RTB Press, 2018).

Biblical Principles for Successful Living

Unfortunately, many people who do not believe are happy to raise a spiritual dilemma, such as "Why do good people suffer?" When there's no immediate answer, they will then declare that there must not be a God. How short-sighted, given the ramifications of such a hasty conclusion. Some individuals may draw these conclusions, in part, to justify living an unconstrained life — one free of any moral or eternal considerations.

Of all the holy books, the Bible offers the most compelling and supportable case for who God is. Please do this assessment for yourself. When it comes to fulfilled prophecy, there is a plethora of evidence to support belief in the Judeo-Christian God. The Bible speaks of the reestablishment of the nation of Israel thousands of years before it occurred. The Bible foretold the birth, birthplace, life, and death of Christ hundreds of years before He arrived on the scene. Micah 5:2, which was written 700 years before Christ, reads, "But you, Bethlehem Ephrata, though you are little among the thousands of Judah, yet out of you shall come forth to Me the one to be Ruler in Israel, whose goings forth are from of old, from everlasting."

Another interesting passage is Isaiah Chapter 53, which vividly and prophetically describes the crucifixion of Jesus centuries before He was ever born. Isaiah 9:6, written in 700 BC, states: "For unto us a Child is born, unto us a Son is given; and the government will be upon His shoulder. And His name will be called Wonderful, Counselor, Mighty God, Everlasting Father, and Prince of Peace."

> **Zechariah 9:9:** "Rejoice greatly, O daughter of Zion! Shout, O daughter of Jerusalem! Behold, your King is coming to you; He is just and having salvation, lowly and riding on a donkey, a colt, the foal of a donkey."

Such are just a few of the many prophecies in Old Testament Scripture that were either initially or sequentially fulfilled by Christ according to New Testament writers and, in many cases, also secular historians.[6]

---

[6] 351 Old Testament Prophecies Fulfilled in Jesus Christ
https://www.newtestamentchristians.com/bible-study-resources/351-old-testament-prophecies-fulfilled-in-jesus-christ/.

The physical and archeological evidence proving statements and events found in the Bible is extensive[7]. There are plenty of resources you can use to verify this for yourself. The field is called *biblical* or *Christian apologetics*, and resources are plentiful. In our courts, we convict people based on evidence and the testimony of eyewitnesses. While we cannot physically duplicate or see for ourselves the resurrection of Christ, according to Scripture there were hundreds of eyewitnesses who did see Christ after the resurrection.

The life and death of Jesus Christ are attested by many secular historians.[8] Among the eyewitnesses were the apostles, who wrote most of the Gospels and Epistles we find in the New Testament. Their bold testimony to the gospel of Jesus Christ — to what they had witnessed in His life, ministry, death, and resurrection — put their very lives at risk. If you have doubts, take time to read up on it and convince yourself. I recommend Dr. Josh McDowell's *Evidence that Demands a Verdict*. You could also watch or read some of Lee Strobel's compelling apologetic works.

Many of the disciples died a martyr's death. Peter was the first to confess Jesus as "the Christ, the Son of the living God" (Matthew 16:16) — yet later he denied three times that he even knew the Lord (see Matthew 26:70–74). Still, after His resurrection, Jesus forgave Peter, and he continued as an important apostle who would help build the Church and who was eventually martyred for Christ.[9]

Several apostles who were martyred may have had an opportunity to declare that Christ's resurrection was fake, which might have saved their lives; but they elected not to do so. Why? What had they seen? They had seen the life, death, and resurrection of God incarnate — Jesus Christ.[10] And they had been empowered by receiving His Holy Spirit at Pentecost.

---

[7] Paul L Maier. Biblical Archaeology: Factual Evidence to Support the Historicity of the Bible. http://www.equip.org/article/biblical-archaeology-factual-evidence-to-support-the-historicity-of-the-bible/.

[8] The Historical Record of Jesus Life from Secular Sources. https://robertcliftonrobinson.com/2014/05/11/the-historical-record-of-jesus-life-from-secular-sources/.

[9] Sean McDowell, Was Peter Crucified Upside Down? https://seanmcdowell.org/blog/was-peter-crucified-upside-down.

[10] Sean McDowell, Were the Apostles Willing to Die for a Misguided Faith? https://seanmcdowell.org/blog/were-the-apostles-of-jesus-misguided.

Biblical Principles for Successful Living

Humankind has a propensity to think God should be all things to all people and that He should allow any path to Him that seems right to them. But, just as the Internal Revenue Service, your employer, or anyone else in authority has a set of rules, regulations, and standards, God also has His. God's rule is that you come to Him through the sacrifice of Jesus Christ his Son — and you do so by faith. The good news is that anyone can do this. Contrary to most religious systems, Christianity says that you cannot obtain salvation through your own actions and good works. If you could do so, then Christ came to earth to suffer and die in vain. Christ's sacrifice applies past, present, and future from the cross. He is the only way people of all times and generations will be finally reconciled to God.

Who gets to go to heaven? According to the Bible, salvation and eternal security are granted through faith in Jesus Christ to *whosoever will believe on Him*. The thing that appeals to people about most popular religions is how difficult they are to follow. Many people think the more difficult the required religious ritual is, the more likely it is that a particular religion will get you to heaven. All the trappings and discipline of religion can provide much comfort and false assurance. True Christianity, however, asserts that there is no comfort or assurance other than through humble faith in Christ Himself. It results in a realization that you are totally dependent upon the sacrifice of Christ, no matter how good you believe yourself to be.

Fundamentally, most religions involve man reaching up, trying to find and impress God. These can be considered works-based theologies, in which a man or woman hopes to earn salvation by being a good person and doing good things. Christianity stands in stark opposition to that approach. Christianity is God reaching down to find man. Christianity is God giving His very own Son to pay the penalty for sin (death) that we could not pay, to appease His own perfect and sinless nature. We need to believe in and accept the sacrifice of Jesus Christ and the person of Jesus Christ for our salvation. His death paid our sin debt, and His righteousness became our righteousness. We stand "born again" before God when we believe.

How people can look at this world and not clearly see the evidence of two opposing spiritual forces is hard to understand. One can look at the good works of Mother Teresa or Billy Graham, for example, and contrast them with the terrible deeds of Hitler, Mao, or Stalin. All of these human beings have submitted themselves to the thoughts, ideas, and methods of either God or Satan. In life, we can see God in the good; and we can see Satan, the enemy of our souls, in the bad. And we all make that choice as well to one degree or another each and every day. The world's system is based on selfishness. Satan is the god of this world. The Kingdom of God is based on love and selflessness. Faith operating through love is the key.

How can you be an atheist when, by far, the safest course of action is to believe? When one does the analysis, it's easy to see that if you believe, then you are sure to come out ahead. It goes something like this: If you do believe, and there is a God, then you win, because you are on God's team; and if you do believe, and there is not a God, then you win based on the quality of life you enjoyed while being alive from following good, biblical principles. If you don't believe and there is not a God, then you may have lived a less satisfying life; but you don't end up apart from God. And, finally, if you don't believe and there is a God, then you lose big in eternity. So the only clearly losing proposition is not to believe in God.

You may say that if I believe and live according to God's rules, then I will not live a fulfilling and rewarding life. This is a fallacy. All one needs to do is engage in behaviors considered biblically sinful a few times to realize that such behaviors do not lead to lasting fulfillment, peace of mind, or physical health. Nor do they bless others whom you may have negatively impacted. Such behaviors may result in temporary satisfaction or apparent happiness, but in the long run, they will amount to little or nothing and will certainly leave you a poor legacy.

The Bible is an amazing book. Even for the most imaginative author, it would be difficult to make up the things that are in the Bible. One of most impressive features of the Bible is that pictures of Christ can be found throughout. A compelling example of this comes from comparing Genesis and Leviticus to the book of Hebrews. Genesis and Leviticus were written long before our Savior Jesus came to earth, and yet He can be seen symbolically in the establishment of two priesthoods: those of Melchizedek and of the Levites.

S. Michael Houdmann discusses the significance of these priesthoods in his book *Questions About Jesus Christ: The 100 Most Frequently Asked Questions About Jesus Christ*. In Genesis 14, before the Law was passed from

Biblical Principles for Successful Living

Moses to the Israelites, we're told that Melchizedek was King of Salem and priest of the Most High God. This priest-king blessed Abraham, and Abraham in response gave Melchizedek a tenth (tithe) of all his spoils from war.

Much later, Abraham's great-grandson Levi was chosen by God to be the father of a tribe of priests, the Levites, who would serve Him and His Tabernacle. These priests were servants of the Tabernacle and Temple and responsible for making intercession to God for the people by offering the many sacrifices that the Law required. One of these priests was selected as the High Priest, and he alone could enter the Most Holy Place, once a year on the Day of Atonement. There he would offer a sacrifice of blood on the Ark of the Covenant in order to cover the sins of the people (Leviticus 16:11–34; Hebrews 9:7).

With these daily and yearly sacrifices, the sins of the people were temporarily covered until the Messiah would come to take away their sins forever. So, in Hebrews, when Jesus is called our High Priest, this refers to both of these previous priesthoods. Like Melchizedek, Jesus is ordained as a priest apart from the Law given on Mount Sinai (Hebrews 5:6). And like the Levitical priests, Jesus offered a sacrifice of blood to satisfy the Law of God when He offered Himself for our sins (Hebrews 7:26–27). However, unlike the Levitical priests, who had to continually offer sacrifices, Jesus had to offer His sacrifice only once, gaining eternal redemption for all who come to God through Him (Hebrews 9:12).[11]

The Old Testament and the Mosaic Law show us pictures of the Christ throughout. Take the story of Joseph as an example. Joseph was placed into prison and eventually became the number two person in the palace of Egypt under Pharaoh, putting him in the position to save all of his family. In this way, Joseph is a "type" of Christ. In the story of Abraham and Isaac, we see the father, Abraham, willing to give up his son, Isaac, just as God was willing to give up His Son Jesus. As God provided a ram to take the place of Isaac, sparing his life, so God also provided the Lamb of God, His Son, to take our place as the sacrifice for sins and to fulfill the

---

[11] Houdmann, S. M. *Questions About Jesus Christ: The 100 Most Frequently Asked Questions About Jesus Christ.* WestBow Press, 2013.

righteous requirements of God. All we need do is trust Him. These are two of many examples foreshadowing the Messiah Jesus.

What is biblical belief or trust? Many people say they believe. The book of James tells us that the demons "also believe and tremble" (2:19). When we say that we believe in Jesus unto salvation, what does that really mean, and how do we know if we are really believing? Biblical belief is to commit to Jesus and to trust and obey Him. Biblical belief ultimately results in changed actions and lives. You will never be perfect, but you move in that direction very slowly as God changes your heart.

One should always check to see if they are in the faith. First John says that he who believes in God does not sin (see 3:8–9). Most theologians consider that notion of not sinning to mean not engaging in continual, perpetual, and unrepentant sin. Others say that the believer's spirit is sealed after salvation unto the day of redemption, and the spirit part of you in fact cannot sin, no matter your actions. In any case, for a Christian, sin is normally accompanied by the chastisement of God and the correction of God in their spirit. Those who truly know God and who realize His love for us do not wish to sin against Him, nor do they enjoy sin's inevitable consequences and results.

God knew we could not perfectly obey or keep His law. Therefore, He sent Christ to die to pay the penalty for our transgressions. We have an intercessor for the many times in which we fail. That intercessor is Jesus Christ, the Righteous One, who continually cleanses us of all unrighteousness and makes intercession for us and gives us second chances every day. Our sin, therefore, doesn't need to drive us away from God anymore.

Continual and perpetual sin without the feelings of chastisement or remorse may indicate that we do not know God, but sin itself can no longer separate true believers from God because of what Christ did once and for all time. When you know God by simple faith, your sin is cleansed continually (past, present, and future) by the blood of Christ — the Lamb of God, our once-and-for-all sacrifice, and our perpetual intercessor. 1 John 1:7 says, "But if we walk in the light as He is in the light, we have fellowship with one another, and the blood of Jesus Christ His Son cleanses us from all sin."

So, by now, we should realize that there must be a God who designed and created all things. We see much evidence that He is the God of Abraham, Isaac, and Jacob. We see the uniqueness and historicity of the Bible narrative, and we see Jesus as Savior of the world. We come to God for justification by faith, and by faith alone, clinging to and accepting the sacrifice of Jesus Christ, who makes us right with the Father.

After salvation, many Christians believe that they must rely on perfect obedience to God's law as a means of keeping their salvation through their good behavior. The book of Galatians, however, tells us repeatedly that we begin our journey by faith and must continue by faith. Our eternal salvation through the blood of Jesus Christ is contingent upon grace based on a true faith and is not contingent on our actions.

Once we are truly born again, our hearts belong to God, and we are children of God by faith. The distinction between being under the Mosaic Law for salvation and being under grace is important. You can be legally faultless and still not be saved. Indeed, "by the deeds of the law no flesh will be justified in His sight, for by the law is the knowledge of sin" (Romans 3:20).

In his article "Could You Keep the Law Perfectly, But Still Not Be Saved?" Dr. Paul M. Elliott points out that even if a person were to perfectly keep every point of the Law, that still would not be enough to place them in right standing before God, because an insurmountable obstacle would remain: our sin nature inherited from Adam. But because of God's great grace, we are saved through faith in Jesus Christ, and all of His righteousness is imputed to us. Elliott continues: "That righteousness is not only Jesus' perfect law-keeping, as marvelous and precious as that is. Christ's righteousness is His inherent perfection as the God-man." And it is ours, by grace through faith. In accordance with 2 Corinthians 5:17, no sin — past, present, or future — is imputed to you any longer once you become a child of God by faith, having appropriated the sacrifice of Christ unto yourself.[12]

Finally, the personal evidence that believers' experience is extensive. Christianity is a living faith, not a religion. It is a vital relationship with the Holy God, who is now accessible to us because of what Christ did. In

---

[12] Dr Paul Elliott. "Could You Keep the Law Perfectly, But Still Not Be Saved?" Teaching the Word Ministries. http://www.teachingtheword.org/apps/articles/?articleid=64879&view=post&blogid=5436.

William Lake

the Old Testament, only the high priest could approach God, and that was only once a year. Christ is now our High Priest, and we have free and full access to God the Father through Him. Christianity is not a religion; it is a relationship, a way of life, and a journey. Those who embark on it will have a testimony of a living, interactive relationship with the sovereign Creator of the universe, and that relationship will never be boring.

A quick word about the precious Holy Spirit of God. Many people believe that you get the Holy Spirit separately, sometime after salvation; but it is very clear in the Bible that the Holy Spirit living in you is who makes you a Christian and marks you as a child of God for all eternity. The Bible says that upon salvation, you receive the Holy Spirit. The Bible also says that if you are saved, then the Holy Spirit of God lives in you and seals you for all eternity. If you are a Christian, you have the Holy Spirit in you now to guide you and comfort you.

The fullness of the Holy Spirit comes from yielding to the Holy Spirit. Speaking in tongues and all the gifts of the Spirit come from yielding fully to the indwelling of the Holy Spirit of God. Some teachers say that there is a separate infilling of the Holy Spirit after salvation, which then results in the gift of tongues and the manifestation of certain other gifts. This is often called the Baptism of the Holy Spirit. I would not dispute this, and it is great to pray for this. I would simply say that if you are not walking in the fullness of the power of God's Holy Spirit, then seek His Spirit and His gifts diligently.

A famous Christian pastor by the name of Dr. Henry Allen ("Harry") Ironside was challenged by an agnostic to a public debate. The plan was that the agnostic would present the case for agnosticism, and Dr. Ironside would present the case for Christianity. Dr. Ironside agreed to have the debate, but he had one condition. He told the agnostic that he would debate him in public forum gladly, but the agnostic had to bring with him one man and one woman whose lives were changed for the better through the application of agnosticism. He told the agnostic that he, as a Christian, would in turn provide at least 100 people whose lives were permanently changed for the better through the blood of Jesus Christ and the hope and faith that Christianity gives. The agnostic declined, and the debate never took place.[13]

---

[13] Wikipedia Contributors, "Harry A. Ironside," *Wikipedia, The Free Encyclopedia*, https://en.wikipedia.org/w/index.php?title=Harry_A._Ironside&oldid=855816057.

Chapter 5

What's Your Purpose for Being Here?

Habakkuk 2:2–3: "'Then the Lord answered me and said: 'Write the vision and make it plain on tablets, that he may run who reads it. For the vision is yet for an appointed time; but at the end it will speak, and it will not lie. Though it tarries, wait for it; because it will surely come, it will not tarry.'"

Psalm 100:2: "Serve the Lord with gladness; come before His presence with singing."

Matthew 22:37–40: "Jesus said to him, 'You shall love the Lord your God with all your heart, with all your soul, and with all your mind.' This is the first and great commandment. And the second is like it: 'You shall love your neighbor as yourself.' On these two commandments hang all the Law and the Prophets."

Ephesians 2:10: "For we are His workmanship, created in Christ Jesus for good works, which God prepared beforehand that we should walk in them."

As a young boy, John tended toward being overweight and had a noticeable case of acne. He associated with the kids in his neighborhood, and most of his encounters were healthy, involving rigorous physical exertion in the form of neighborhood football and stick ball games — as well as the typical making of tree forts and having green apple fights. As they got a bit older, however, some of the kids in the neighborhood exposed him to pornography and even tried to get him to try certain drugs.

During his early years in public grammar school and junior high school, John was often bullied because of his portly appearance and his acne. Even the teachers occasionally made fun of him because his pants were too tight and his shirt kept coming out. The older girls made a point of whistling and making cat calls when he walked by, saying, "There goes the hunk" — and other painful remarks. During high school, John tried out and was selected to play on the high school football team. He threw himself into the game and had good success, though he had never played before. He felt he was proving himself to the world and that he was no longer the short, fat, ugly kid that people laughed at and beat up.

The need to prove himself and to be accepted never really left John. As the time for college approached, he began to wonder if his life had a purpose and what he would do for a career. Would his life be special at all? Did he have a unique calling and purpose from God in this life, or should he just pick something he thought he might like to do, and do it for a living? "I want to show them all," he thought to himself. "I will become somebody special that people won't make fun of."

Once you have determined that there is a God, and you have determined who God is and how to approach Him, and you have become His child, determine your purpose for being on earth. People who believe they have a special purpose in life are more likely to work hard and persevere to be successful. As children of God, we find some general purposes for all of our lives listed in Scripture, but there is also God's specific purpose for each person.

Galatians 2:10, quoted above, says we have been called to perform good works He has prepared for us before the beginning of time. Psalm 139:16 says: "Your eyes saw my substance, being yet unformed. And in Your book they all were written, the days fashioned for me, when as yet there were none of them."

Our main purpose in life is to serve God, trust in the Lord, and do good, seeking to make a positive difference in this world, no matter what our vocation. We are to bless others and be the hands and feet of God on earth. In doing so, we store up treasure in heaven and build a lasting legacy. But what exactly is the specific task you are supposed to accomplish? There is no book in the Bible which tells you exactly what profession to choose in your life. You can seek your specific purpose by asking God for a *rhema* word, which is a word specifically for you, from Him.[14]

King Solomon was the richest man in the world. It is said that he had more horses and cattle, and more gold and silver, than any other person who ever lived. He also had 700 wives and 300 concubines. He leaves us with a very interesting conclusion found in the book of Ecclesiastes about the most important thing in life in his opinion.

Ecclesiastes 12:13–14 reads:" Let us hear the conclusion of the whole matter: fear God and keep His commandments, for this is man's all. For God will bring every work into judgment, including every secret thing, whether good or evil."

The Ten Commandments in the Old Testament (Exodus 20:3–17) give a portion of the moral law, which was given to God's people because of their transgressions. The Law serves both as our instructions for living a God-fearing life and as a tutor to show us our need for Christ as Savior, since we cannot fulfill the Law perfectly and are fundamentally imperfect. This shows us our need for Christ.

The first four commandments are dedicated to the relationship between God and man (vertical). The remaining six commandments are designed to tell man how to live with his fellow man (horizontal). Christ was our supreme example, showing us how to follow and fulfill God's law. His explanation in Matthew 5 of what it requires to fully keep God's commandments makes it clear that it is impossible for us to do so in our own human strength; and since even one sin is enough to violate the whole Law, according to James 2:10, we see our need for grace and a Savior.

Jesus boiled down the commandments to two. Mark 12:28–31 tells us that the most important commandment, also called the "royal law," is to love God with all your heart, soul, mind, and strength; and, secondly, to love your neighbor as yourself. The keeping of this commandment by

---

[14] Wikipedia Contributors, "Rhema," *Wikipedia, The Free Encyclopedia,* https://en.wikipedia.org/wiki/Rhema.

an individual will fulfill all the Law. We are to be joyful, love God, and serve our fellow man. When we focus exclusively on ourselves, we will probably be unhappy, discouraged, depressed, and lonely. An old favorite Christian song sums up all of Christian theology in a few words:

> **Trust and obey, for there's no other way**
> **To be happy in Jesus, but to trust and obey.**[15]

How does a person find their specific purpose? You can begin by looking at your talents, gifts, and interests. Romans 11:29 says: "For the gifts and the calling of God are irrevocable" — meaning that they do not change and that God will not revoke them. Assessing these God-given skills and talents — along with your predominant interests, which are very important — can help you determine your life's best purpose.

Galatians 5:22–23 teaches us that the fruits of the spirit are given to all believers. These fruits are love, joy, peace, patience, kindness, goodness, gentleness, meekness, and self-control. Spiritual gifts, on the other hand, are given to each individual according to God's will, and they can also be sought after. 1 Corinthians 12:7–10 says that spiritual gifting includes wisdom, knowledge, faith, healing, miraculous powers, prophecy, distinguishing between spirits, speaking in different kinds of tongues, and the interpretation of tongues. Another scripture, Ephesians 4:11–13, states that God has placed in the church, first of all, apostles; second, prophets; third, teachers; then miracles; gifts of healing; gifts of helping; gifts of guidance; and the gift of different kinds of tongues.

There are many books on the topic of discovering your life's purpose, calling, or profession. Assess your spiritual gifts — your skills, talents, and interests — to find clues to what you are best suited for. What do you love to do? What do you think God planted inside of you? One common question is "What would you want to do for your profession, even if money were no object?" Would you like to be a builder, doctor, lawyer, teacher? Which one has that special ring to it for you?

The *logos* is the written word in the Bible which applies to everyone.

---

[15] John H. Sammis. Trust and Obey. Timeless Truths Free Online Library | books, sheet music, midi, and more. http://library.timelesstruths.org/music/Trust_and_Obey/.

However, when each believer seeks the face of God in prayer, they should seek to receive a special personal or *rhema* word. A *rhema* — in Greek, literally "utterance" or "thing said" — is a word from God specifically for you, given by His Holy Spirit. It should come from the word of God. Listen carefully to God. Seek Him diligently on this. Spend time listening to God when you pray, and then you will discern the *rhema* purpose for your life. The overarching message of *logos* is that you are saved to live for and serve God and your fellow man, no matter what your profession, but you can also seek a specific word as well for what you should do with your life.

I once heard Dr. Mike Murdoch, a great wisdom teacher, say you might pick a profession or at least a ministry focus supported by your main profession which solves a problem that bothers you. Do you know what that might be for you? Perhaps it is educating people, curing the sick, or helping young people to achieve their purpose in spite of poverty or lack of opportunity. Maybe it is ministering the gospel to people locally or around the world, or meeting the needs of orphaned children.

When seeking to hear from God, focus on His love for you and His willingness to help you. Become firmly convinced that God loves you and wants to help you achieve your purpose. Remove static from your reception. Static comes from fear, doubt, guilt, condemnation, sin, lack of forgiveness, and many other sources. Remove them all.

Assess your motives when you decide you want to accomplish something in life. The Bible says that good works are only good in God's sight when they are done for the proper reasons or with proper motives. The choosing of your vocation in life should be done for the right reasons. You may want to be the CEO of a company, but perhaps the reason you want to be a CEO is to validate yourself and feel that you are important — perhaps after a childhood, like John's, in which you felt inferior or were told you would not amount to very much. Your profession should give God the glory and should be the one you can best excel at.

The best and only way to obtain a lasting sense of self-esteem or self-worth is through trusting God's acceptance of you, and in believing what He says about you. Ideally, your career should flow from the gifts and calling of God and your innermost desires and interests, not your desire to prove or validate yourself to others.

I've heard the military phrase that "no plan survives the first contact, so execute violently." Once you determine your purpose, you must then act to bring it about by using good life principles. God has an enemy, and we must use spiritual weapons to fight against him, such as those detailed in Ephesians, Chapter 6, describing the full armor of God.

> **Ephesians 6:12–13:** "For we do not wrestle against flesh and blood, but against principalities, against powers, against the rulers of the darkness of this age, against spiritual hosts of wickedness in the heavenly places. Therefore, take up the whole armor of God that you may be able to withstand in the evil day, and having done all, to stand."

Jesus said: "The thief does not come except to steal, and to kill, and to destroy. I have come that they may have life, and that they may have it more abundantly" (John 10:10).

Jesus told his followers to go and preach the gospel to the ends of the earth, making disciples of all nations. If the vision you discern for your life has something to do with making the world a better place, helping develop people, helping the poor and needy, and spreading the gospel, then you can be sure God's power and provision will be there for you and will sustain you and protect you. Tie your resources and your plans to God's purposes, and He will empower you to succeed. An easy way to do this: In any profession in which you find yourself, be a lover and encourager of people, a generous giver, and a fervent pray-er. These will tie you in nicely to God's purposes.

Summarizing: Your general purpose as a Christian is to trust the Lord, do good to all, and serve Him in all the ways you can — including praying, giving, and serving others. Strive to be a person of character and excellence that others can emulate, leading others to Christ, first by your example, then by your words. Seek to raise godly children for the kingdom, give generously to the church and the poor, and do good for all you can when opportunities arise.

Your specific purpose and how you will spend your life are decisions between you and God. Finding your purpose should be based on your gifting, talents, interests, and inclinations. Whatever it is, dedicate it to God. Do it all for God's glory and for the love of others, and He will empower your success. You want to position your life where He wants you and where He is working, as that is where He will bless you most. Be attentive to the indwelling Holy Spirit, who is your gift from God as a Christian. Let Him be your guide into all of God's purposes for you.

Chapter 6
You Are Thinking Your Future Now!

Isaiah 55:8: "For My thoughts are not your thoughts, nor are your ways, My ways, says the Lord."

Philippians 4:8: "Finally, brethren, whatever things are true, whatever things are noble, whatever things are just, whatever things are pure, whatever things are lovely, whatever things are of good report, if there is any virtue and if there is anything praiseworthy — meditate on these things."

John got married shortly after graduation from college after a brief courtship. He never really learned much about being an effective husband or father from Scripture or good mentors. He began a life with his new spouse, occasionally attending church. He and his wife usually went out to dinner every night after work, not concerning themselves with saving money for the future or contingencies. They ran up credit card debt and usually spent most of what they earned. John did not really have a clear vision for the future and was not steering his family in any particular direction. John never thought much about controlling his thoughts — or even that he should manage his thoughts now to plan, create, and pursue a better future.

For John, God and religion were just a list of do's and don'ts, not connected to daily activities or success. He had faith in God and believed he was "saved," but never tied his faith or the Bible's wisdom to his daily routine or his planning processes. He did not give much thought to his legacy. He continued to struggle with his weight, always seeing himself as overweight and unattractive. This caused him to seek affirmation from everyone he met. John believed life was to be lived without a lot of unnecessary planning. "Think about what's going on now, and it will all work out. Thoughts today don't have much impact on the future," he thought. Planning, saving, and leading the family to a visualized future were not high on his list.

Everyone should monitor and control their thoughts carefully. The thought life is the breeding ground of the future and the fertile soil for the reality we are slowly creating. When we become Christians, the Bible tells us the Holy Spirit of God dwells in us and will guide us if we are attentive and listen to His still, small voice. The devil will always seek to use his weapons of destructive thoughts and ideas to influence us in the wrong direction. The Christian life is letting Christ live through us by dying to self.

> **Galatians 2:20:** "I have been crucified with Christ; it is no longer I who live, but Christ lives in me; and the life which I now live in the flesh I live by faith in the Son of God, who loved me and gave Himself for me."

What you do, what you say, the choices you make, and what you become, all begin in your mind. The first step to something becoming reality occurs in the mind. We should ask ourselves if employing a particular thought pattern is going to get us where we ultimately want to go. If we have determined our life's purpose, we can easily answer that question. Ask yourself if a certain thought pattern, meditation, or visualization increases or decreases your chances of reaching the goals you have established. Does it make you feel happy or sad? Does it inspire you to action or discourage you? Does it energize you or exhaust you? If the thought is not a positive, productive, or helpful one, then you should get rid of it and not dwell on it.

We have several great weapons in the war of the mind. One weapon is the simple fact that the mind cannot think about two things at the same time. We get to choose what we think about, how long we think about it, and what we do with it. We have the choice of replacing a bad or troublesome thought with a good or peaceful thought — or continuing to dwell on the harmful thought. When struggling with a destructive thought, we have the alternative choice of thinking about God, meditating on relevant Scripture verses, or speaking the Word of God out loud.

Using words to overcome thoughts can be very effective also, as self-talk is very powerful. You can focus on only one thing at a time. Self-talk is more powerful than other talk. It is unfortunate that most self-talk, in my experience, is negative.

Everything you do starts with an idea or a thought, so we need to choose our predominant ideas and beliefs wisely, because they will drive our actions. How can you know what is true? All that is necessary is to accept the truths in the Word of God. Believe about yourself and your future only what the Word of God says. Meditate on — don't just read — the Word of God. Form a desired life-picture in your mind that matches what Scripture allows. In order for the power of the truth in the Word of God to become manifest in your life, you must go beyond simply reading the Word of God. Focus on the Word until those truths become very real to you. Your faith will grow, and you will begin to more routinely expect positive results.

The power of an idea should be obvious to everyone. Ideas drive all behaviors. There are many wrong ideas people accept which create wrong and misguided behaviors. *Although people die, ideas live on after them.* We have several examples of powerful ideas that have driven destructive behaviors long after their initiators were gone. Ideas such as Nazism, racial superiority, communism, evolution, and certain radical or extremist religious groups or factions have certainly taken their toll on humanity, and they continue to do so today.

Many think the theory of evolution put forward by Darwin implied that certain races of people were inferior to others.[16] These ideas have driven racist behaviors — such as those exhibited by Hitler against Jews or people of color — and slavery in its many forms. There was a time during the Crusades when Christians wrongfully hated the Jewish people and went to war against them, believing that they were responsible for

---

[16] Dr. Jerry Bergman. Darwinism and the Nazi Race Holocaust. https://answersingenesis.org/charles-darwin/racism/darwinism-and-the-nazi-race-holocaust/.

the death of Christ. Wrong ideas drive wrong actions. Ideas and beliefs are fundamentally and critically important. Be careful what you accept as your source of truth and the ideas you choose to believe.

Romans, Chapter 4, tells us that we believers are the seed of Abraham because the true seed of Abraham are all the children of God by faith (see verses 1–3 and 16–22). Read Romans and Galatians for complete treatises on justification by faith. We are entitled to the same blessings as Abraham's lineage. Abraham's faith was reckoned unto him as righteousness. Indeed, the Scriptures make clear that righteousness has always been by faith.

> **Galatians 3:24–26:** "Therefore the law was our tutor to bring us to Christ, that we might be justified by faith. But after faith has come, we are no longer under a tutor. For you are all sons of God through faith in Christ Jesus."
>
> **Titus 2:11–12:** "For the grace of God that brings salvation has appeared to all men, teaching us that, denying ungodliness and worldly lusts, we should live soberly, righteously, and godly in the present age."

The Law was given to be a tutor to lead us to Christ and was added because of transgressions, but salvation and righteousness before God have always been by faith. **So, if your belief systems are proper, you realize that you are saved by grace through faith as a free gift. You realize that God loves you and wants only the best for you. He does not want to punish you or make you miserable, and He absolutely does want to bless you. He wants you to love Him as He loves you.**

You should know that, as a Christian, God is with you in times of trouble to help you, to redeem and grow you — He is not waiting to punish you or judge you. You should agree with God and what He says about you, and you should expect only the best from Him. This is a true and comforting mental framework from which to view the world. Your success is up to you, and it all starts in the mind. There will be obstacles along the way. However, God promises never to leave you or forsake you. What goes on between your ears is critical to your success.

It has been said that what you see depends on what you look for. Your reality is shaped by the framework within your mind, for through it you interpret everything you see around you. This framework comes from your life experiences and training. Adam and Eve, in the very beginning, did not have any prejudices or faulty belief systems, hang-ups, guilt trips, condemnation, bad experiences, childhood abuse, or dysfunctional television shows! Those of us — everyone — who grew up in imperfect families, and who were victims of imperfect choices and an imperfect world with sinful patterns embedded throughout, have developed many negative mental filters through which our minds interpret things and process the world.

It is best if we interpret the meaning or intent behind what a person says based more upon what they actually say than on facial expression or body language. Often we assess a person's appearance, demographics, facial expressions, or any of their mannerisms in order to interpret what they are thinking and the meaning behind what they are saying — even before a word is spoken. Such interpretations are not always accurate. We may interpret something someone says as harsh because they have a scowl on their face; but it may be that they have a scowl on their face because of something that happened at home that morning, or maybe that's just the way their face looks. Give people the benefit of the doubt by expecting or believing the best.

Be careful to properly establish your personal worldview by using the Word of God and not exclusively your experiences. You can live in a certain place in your mind, regardless of actual reality. You can create your reality with your perceptions. You can see bad in good things and good in bad things. You can be happy in a bad situation or sad in a good situation — and it will all be in your mind. People who have been overweight all their lives may always see themselves as fat, even if they have lost weight. People who have been treated unfairly at one point in their lives based on religion, national origin, race, or any other characteristic or experience, may tend to sense similarly motivated unfairness in every negative interaction, whether it is the real cause or not. Expect the best, and you may get it.

Students will often give up on a subject and not study that subject because of one bad event during which they told themselves — or someone else told them — that they were not capable of doing well in it. In that case, they may not study that subject much anymore, and it becomes virtually certain that they will never become proficient in it — not because they lacked aptitude but because of the lack of further effort. Those who have experienced repeated failures may come to expect failure and may unwittingly drive all future results in that direction by what they say and do — or what they do not say or do. The mind is very powerful.

Your thought processes can totally exhaust you and take away your desire to continue if you let them. The forces of evil attack our minds by injecting wrong thoughts. They also attack our minds by distracting us with fundamentally good, yet less than perfect, things — and driving those things to excess in our lives. One of the easiest ways for our lives to become derailed is with the excess of essentially good things like food, sex, or even religion.

The mind can play many tricks. When people get tired, their minds are more susceptible to being tricked. Don't make important decisions when tired, sad, or angry. The mind and the ideas that drive it are responsible for the greatest achievements and the greatest failures of our lives. Choose carefully what you believe and what you think, as they drive you to your future choices.

Another popular lie is that if our parents were divorced, or if our families were dysfunctional, then we don't have as good a chance of success in life as others do. This is ludicrous. No one has a perfect life. Everybody has baggage and negative experiences to work through. Success or failure will, in the end, be the result of your choices. Guard your mind and treat it as a garden. Pull the weeds out of it and let grow and flourish only those things which have a God-ordained purpose.

One example in the Bible that makes this point powerfully is the story of Josiah, who at the age of eight became King of Judah during the time when the southern and northern kingdoms were divided (see 2 Kings 22:1–2). He was the grandson of Manasseh, one of the more evil kings in the history of God's people. Manasseh's son, Amon, was Josiah's father, and he also did evil in the sight of God, according to Scripture. Despite this unimpressive lineage, little Josiah grew to become one of the kings in the history of the southern kingdom of Judah who pleased God greatly. Josiah is a testimony to the fact that your genetics or your family example do not need to determine your choices or your future.

Another point to remember is that, as Christians, our bloodline is now spiritually through Jesus Christ. The Holy Spirit and the Word of God are our mentors, leading us into successful paths. With Christ as our Savior and brother, God as our Father, and the Holy Spirit sealing us as children of God, we are adopted into a great family lineage, indeed. And we can be mentored by this wonderful family through reading the Word of God in the Bible and heeding the Spirit within.

Don't be discouraged when bad or limiting thoughts or ideas come into your mind. Be diligent to remove those thoughts and replace them with good, biblical thoughts. When you wake up in the morning worrying or feeling fearful, you don't have to continue that thought pattern by dwelling on those thoughts or beginning your day by speaking those things that trouble you. You can realize the path that those thoughts are leading you on is not a productive one, and you can stop the thoughts by countering them with truths from the Word of God. These truths don't change.

We should direct our thoughts, speech, and efforts toward the positive outcome of honoring God and reaching the goals we set for our lives. Knowing that the thoughts we think and speak are directly connected to our actions and subsequent outcomes — negative to negative, positive to positive — it becomes clear that maintaining positive thoughts, mental pictures, and speech is essential to reaching our goals. Therefore, we must be diligent in our thought life to nurture the positive and banish the negative.

What we believe is critically important to going forward in our Christian lives. Do you believe God loves you and has provided for healing and provision as well as salvation at the cross? Does God still do miracles? Does God hear and act on our prayers? Can we accomplish whatever we put our minds to? Will God tell me what He wants me to do in life if I ask? Does He care about me and love me? Is God merciful and kind, and has His hatred of evil and sin been satisfied with the sacrifice of His precious Son?

Thankfully, the answer to each of these questions is a resounding *yes*. Believe it and live like you believe it. God desires to work good into your life and prosper you in the paths He has planned for you.

Do you think God will guide you if you ask Him to? How does one know if God is speaking to them? I have found that when God speaks,

He places an instruction or a desire into my heart or mind that I may not at first even know is from Him. He does not condemn or confuse but, rather, offers a course of action very gently. Most of the time for me, a thought comes to mind such as "go there" or "do this," and I obey it, not realizing until later that it is from God. In accordance with Psalm 37:4, if you delight yourself in the Lord, if you seek your happiness in God, **the Lord will give you — place into you — the desire of your heart that you will then act on.**

This is in stark contrast to the devil, who confuses, condemns, and seeks to destroy. For big issues, when discerning whether what you hear in your heart or mind is from God, check the Word of God. It is also wise to seek the counsel of several of your most godly associates who are familiar with the Word and who know you and your issue. If a course of action is not clearly against Scripture, and it is in your heart to do it, and wise counsel supports it, then it is likely good to do. The Bible speaks of a time when the prophet Elijah sought to hear from God while in a cave (see 1 Kings 19). God spoke to Elijah in a still small voice rather than the wind, earthquake, and fire he observed. Sometimes, when God whispers, we don't even know it is He.

The Bible tells us that God wants to meet all of our needs, and that He wants us to have joy on earth, even though it is sometimes difficult because of a fallen world. God's desire for us is seen in His desire for Adam and Eve before the fall. God wanted Adam and Eve to live in health, having eternal life in close fellowship with Him, without sin, pain, suffering, or disease. Of course, sin entered the world and changed all that, but God still wants the same good things for us.

We must agree with God in faith in our thoughts and speaking patterns that He will bring His desired results to pass. The Bible tells us to speak those things that are not as though they were. If one thinks and speaks sickness and poverty, they will likely encounter those things in life because thought and speech affect choices. It's not mystical. It's just that if you don't feel that you will receive opportunities from God, you will simply not look for them — or take advantage of them if they appear. Words can also open doors to evil, and you can influence your own body with them. This is not magic or New Age theology. The mind is very connected to our emotions, actions, and bodies, and can affect our lives.

As far as monetary prosperity goes, God is a lavish God. The description of heaven is full of gold, pearls, and precious jewels. The description of God's temple, as He instructed Solomon to build it, was very lavish. Psalm 35:27 says: "Let them shout for joy and be glad, who favor my righteous cause; and let them say continually, let the Lord be magnified, who has pleasure in the prosperity of His servant."

God wants us to have what we need to fulfill His purpose for us, not to simply shower us with so much wealth that we lose our focus on Him as our provider. Money is probably the thing that most easily can replace God in our lives, since it seemingly solves so many problems. Proverbs 30:9 essentially asks God not to give us too little or too much, because either of these can bring trouble. God wants us to have sufficient provision, healthy relationships, healthy bodies, and a healthy mind. God wants the best for His children, just as we parents want the best for our children. The Word is full of what God wants for us, and this is what you must fill your mind with. Let it be the framework through which you interpret the rest of reality and upon which you base your expectations.

Beware of limiting theologies. Expect God to act to accomplish His purposes in your life. Expect to see His promises fulfilled to include the occasional miracle; expect to hear from God; expect God to be active in your life and guide you through the Word and His indwelling Holy Spirit. There is nothing sadder than a religious theology which denies the power of God and results in a negative and critical spirit. Resolve never to go back. Stop waiting for someone else to do it. Yield to the Holy Spirit, never stop dreaming, and know why you are here. To change, you need a desire to change. Stop making excuses and take appropriate action, to change how you see yourself from Satan's picture of you to God's picture of you as revealed in His Word.

A person gets off track when his or her focus is broken by distractions such as sin, worry, or fear. Keep your life free from distractions. Remember that your standing before God is assured through the sacrifice of Christ once you are His. You need not be concerned with the past any longer or any mistakes you may still make insofar as they affect your standing with God. Hebrews 12:1 says, "Therefore we also, since we are surrounded by so great a cloud of witnesses, let us lay aside every weight, and the sin which so easily ensnares us, and let us run with endurance the race that is set before us."

Do not open any door for Satan to enter. One of the common doors Satan uses to enter into someone's life is sin that results from not obeying the Word of God. Such behavior gives Satan the chance to come in with thoughts of fear, doubt, guilt, and condemnation — and their unpleasant natural consequences. Some theologians also believe that Satan gains a legal right to trouble you when you sin. I am not convinced of this, but it is not worth taking any risks. Sin diminishes our all-important faith, focus, and inner peace. The ideas brought in by Satan are what we must guard the mind against. God does not leave us when we sin if we are in Christ. Remember, 1 John 1:7 says, "But if we walk in the light as He is in the light, we have fellowship with one another, and the blood of Jesus Christ His Son cleanses us from all sin."

Satan and his demonic hosts may target you by placing troubling recollections, fears, suggestions, or guilt trips in your mind. Such things are the fiery darts of the enemy, and they attack the mind. In Christ, we are forgiven of all our sin — past, present, and future. However, when we violate the Word of God, we open the door to let in guilt, fear, condemnation, and the negative consequences which frequently come to pass in the natural realm.

The things God is against in our lives are indeed things that we should not do because they are not good for us or our fellow man, and they often bring unpleasant consequences. But we must remember in any case not to walk in fear and not to feel condemned. Just begin to do the next right thing and refuse to dwell on painful thoughts. Force your mind to move on to something else. This takes discipline, but it is a most helpful skill. Remember, God gives an instruction and a desire, not a beating. If you get an overwhelming urge to do something that is contrary to Scripture, do not be alarmed. Just accept the fact that these desires are still present on occasion, reject them, and move on to the next thought or action.

Our expectations can also affect our mental outlook and disposition. When expectations are not met or are delayed, discouragement can creep in. Proverbs 13:12 tells us that "hope deferred makes the heart sick." Be careful that you do not create false expectations for yourself or in what you expect from others. Only God can fulfill all of your needs. You can always expect good from the hand of God and not evil — depend on Him to *always* give exceedingly and immeasurably more than what you ask or imagine. You should not expect much from others — by nature they, like all of us, are limited and fallible. Give much and expect little in return.

Remember that good things always take time. It may take months to form new habits and see their results. It is better to start good habits well in advance of negative manifestations. For example, many people will pray for healing, but they will not establish the good habits necessary, such as prayer, exercise, and diet, to avoid health trouble in the first place.

Another factor for a proper mental outlook is forgiveness, which is as much for the person doing the forgiving as it is for the one who needs forgiveness. Harboring resentment and unforgiveness is like a cancer to your well-being. The sin of unforgiveness is a poison that pollutes your spirit. Biblical principles help us tend the garden of our mind. Scripture tells us to love and forgive everyone, even our enemies. Love does no harm, and it overlooks an offense. If we have anger or lack of forgiveness in our hearts, we are told to release it in favor of love. This will actually restore focus and cause the mind and body to function better. This especially includes forgiving yourself.

Do not be afraid to work hard — and even fail — because all good things take time and effort and generally start slowly. The fear of failure will prevent you from trying and realizing a possibly great result. Learn to take God at His word, and the sooner the better. Learn from other people's mistakes. Do not make the same mistake more than once if at all possible. Negative events can also change your thinking patterns and change who you are over time if you let them.

Fear is a joy-killer. Be able to recognize a fear thought as being in opposition to the guidance of the Holy Spirit who lives within you. A fear thought normally comes into your mind and gives you a strong, loud, negative emotional reaction. The voice of God, however, is a still small voice that very often we tend to discount or ignore. When you understand what a fear thought feels like, recognize it, know that it's not from God, and reject it. Thoughts and ideas that God puts into your mind are normally gentle, redemptive in nature, and bring about repentance, not discouragement. His thoughts normally do not cause great discomfort but, rather, eventually become a desire in your heart to do the right thing (see Psalm 37:4). Everything Jesus did in Scripture was redemptive.

Be open to change and personal development. It is hard to change.

Often other people give us the best input, but we must be willing to accept it. It can come from anyone, anywhere, so be ready. And do not discount a word of wisdom because you do not think the source is "good enough." You never know where God's wisdom will come from.

Pride also hinders. "By pride comes nothing but strife," says Proverbs 13:10, "but with the well-advised is wisdom." Pride, self-focus, and becoming easily or often offended will also hinder successful mental achievement. We must be at a state of peace in our minds to reflect God most effectively.

Believe well, because what you believe is very important. From ideas and the mind spring all words and actions — and, eventually, your entire destiny. You must constantly feed your faith and endeavor to live righteously. Dr. Adrian Rogers discusses the importance of fighting for a pure and positive thought life in his article "The Battle of the Mind": "Your enemy, the devil, has ensconced himself in high places to war against you. And there is a deadly, invisible array of demonic hosts dedicated to the destruction of your thought life. Satan's desire is to conquer and control your thought life. But, when God saved you, He gave you the mind of Christ. The devil wants to get your mind because he knows that if he can get your mind, he can pull you away from the Lord Jesus Christ."[17]

Fight hard, because you are in a war. Put on the full armor of God to fight and defeat the devil (see Ephesians 6:11–17). Replace evil thoughts with godly thoughts. The importance of the mind cannot be overstated. Center your mind upon Jesus. Every person has been shaped by their experiences. Sometimes experiences can have negative effects which people may not even realize. Consider these examples:

1. A person who is abused as a child may have trouble trusting God or a mate.
2. A person who has been bullied and rejected may see rejection everywhere they go later in life and find it hard to accept love when it appears.

---

[17] Rogers, Adrian. "The Battle of the Mind." LightSource. https://www.lightsource.com/ministry/love-worth-finding/articles/the-battle-of-the-mind-12826.html. Permission also obtained from Love Worth Finding.

Biblical Principles for Successful Living

3. A person who is or has been overweight may always see themselves in that manner.
4. Persons who have been exposed to abnormal sexual activities, pornography, or childhood abuse may have a distorted image of sex, which can lead to strained marital expectations and dysfunctional comparisons.
5. Those who have experienced much sadness or loss of loved ones may not expect anything other than that. They may feel they are always vulnerable to evil and may have a difficult time expecting good things from the hand of God.
6. Children in poverty may not develop a concept of the future or what they can become when they grow up, or even of growing up at all.
7. People who have been in performance-based situations all of their lives may have a difficult time believing that God or anyone else would value them aside from what they can achieve or how they behave. They may always believe all love is conditional.
8. People who have committed a certain sin or negative action and cannot forgive themselves cannot accept and expect that good things can happen, even after forgiveness — or that God can still use them.
9. A man or woman who has a negative or non-existent father model may find it very difficult to accept God as a loving Father and seek a trusting relationship with Him.
10. A person may fail a few times. This may create a mental attitude of expecting failure in any future endeavor.

Remember, though, that God can use your experiences for good. Depend on Him for your success. Let trials make you better. Negative experiences you have encountered — or even those you see in the news routinely, such as suffering, death, and killing — can affect your mental outlook and change who you are. Unfortunately, some experiences may be very hard to overcome. But God's promises of redemption and second chances still apply, and you can certainly be emotionally healed if you will believe.

God is an expert at bringing good out of bad. He can work through your suffering to accomplish His purposes in your life. Ultimately, God is in control, and we can trust Him to work all things together for good in the lives of those who love Him (see Romans 8:28). If you have experienced the devastating effects of abuse, trauma, tragic loss, or even the horrors of war, and are struggling with their aftermath, God can heal and restore you, and lead you into the great future He has for you. You can do all things through Christ, who strengthens you (Philippians 4:13).

Use your imagination wisely for God. The imagination can be a wonderful tool with which to create a bright future. Your life will go in the direction of your thoughts, so make sure what you meditate on and imagine is carefully monitored. Make sure what you wish for, pray for, and daydream about is directly and positively related to what you want to happen.

Learn the practice of rejecting and removing your negative thoughts and emotions. Reject Satan as he seeks to inject thoughts into your mind that trouble you and cause you to worry. Absolutely refuse to be debilitated by fear, doubt, and worry. Worrying about things you cannot change will exhaust and paralyze you, negatively influence your decisions, and diminish your personal effectiveness. Believe the scriptures that apply to any situation you face and happily realize that God is with you, He is for you, and He will not let you down. Take God at His word and apply His instructions to your life liberally.

Once you are a child of God by faith, rejoice and see yourself as such. Know above all that God loves you. Let your thoughts and perceptions be guided only by the truth found in biblical principles. What is between your ears is the most important thing you possess, so guard it well. Be careful about what goes into your eye and ear gates, and don't limit yourself with persistently negative self-talk. If you are a child of God, anything negative that happens in your life is not the judgment of God; rather, it is something God always desires to turn or use for good. God still loves you and is still with you. Remember and expect that God is still a God of miracles. Nothing has changed. Expect the best that God has and wants to give you as His child.

Chapter 7
How Your Words Help You Achieve Your Goals

James 3:3–5: "Indeed, we put bits in horses' mouths that they may obey us, and we turn their whole body. Look also at ships: although they are so large and are driven by fierce winds, they are turned by a very small rudder wherever the pilot desires. Even so the tongue is a little member and boasts great things."

Matthew 12:36–37: "But I say to you that for every idle word men may speak, they will give account of it in the Day of Judgment. For by your words you will be justified, and by your words you will be condemned."

Proverbs 18:6, 7, 20, 21: "A fool's lips enter into contention. And his mouth calls for blows. A fool's mouth is his destruction and his lips are the snare of his soul. [20]A man's stomach shall be satisfied from the fruit of his mouth; from the produce of his lips he shall be filled. Death and life are in the power of the tongue, and those who love it will eat its fruit."

Luke 8:11: "Now the parable is this: the seed is the Word of God."

John noticed that he wasn't experiencing as many positive results as he desired in his Christian walk. He still had trouble keeping his mind in the "faith zone" and maintaining an attitude of expectancy. His prayers seemed flat and uninspired. He then assessed his daily routine and realized that much of his day was spent complaining with his co-workers or at home. He spoke frequently about nothing in particular, usually with a decidedly negative tone.

John sometimes spoke sarcastically to his children and wife, and he tended to be very critical of others. He did not even realize how negative his casual and off-the-cuff remarks were most of the time. He routinely made critical or negative statements to his wife about their marriage, the kids' behavior, politics, how he physically felt, or his day at work. His words usually expressed a negative outlook rather than a faith-fueled, expectant attitude.

John rarely discussed the future. He bought into the idea that whatever was going to happen in life would happen — and that what he said really did not matter that much. Accordingly, his words reflected his random thoughts, resignation to chance outcomes, and total ignorance of the part he played in verbally creating his future. When he prayed — usually that nothing bad would happen to him or his family, and making several requests for things he wanted — he often later spoke against the likelihood of his prayers being answered. He did this in order to lower his own expectations and avoid disappointments. He wondered if his words really did matter, as some of the preachers he had heard on television said they did, or if the connection between words and life results was purely some New Age concoction that some church people spoke of. He wondered if he could really use his words to change his life.

Now that we have discussed the importance of the mind and our thoughts, let's focus on the words we speak. Words are important. For example, Proverbs 15:1 says that a calm word turns away wrath, but a harsh word stirs up anger. This is a clear example of words triggering reactions in other people, and this in turn impacts us. Words can create the work or family environments we operate in.

We have often heard someone described as a person of few words, generally with respect. I have come to realize over the years that being a person of few words may actually be more effective than being a person of many words. It seems that almost everyone is talking too much these days, while listening very little. I do not think many of us appreciate the value of keeping our mouths shut most of the time.

Learn to say those things that really matter and that have a godly purpose. Following this advice, you substantially increase your probability of being a person of impact. Do not speak idle words. I once heard Dr. Myles Munro say in a sermon that idle words are words which do not have a kingdom purpose. Be quick to listen, slow to speak, and slow to anger. Be quiet, be still, listen, and learn. Speak with power and scriptural authority. Powerful words are powerful because they are true. And where is real truth found? In Scripture.

The Bible says we are made in the image and likeness of God. Insofar as our words agree with the will of God and the Word of God, we can expect our words to carry creative power. However, the positive connection between words and results is not always in effect if the words you are speaking are not based upon scriptural promises, and if you have not reached the point of truly believing or expecting these promises to be fulfilled in your life.

It is important to choose and use your words wisely. Your words tend to influence other people, and they also influence you personally. You can shape what people think of you and what you think of yourself by what you say, whether aloud or in your mind. This in turn impacts your and their actions and expectations and, ultimately, your results. Should you tell your boss that you are not a capable worker? Should you tell your kids they will not amount to much? Should you tell your wife she is a terrible cook? Should you tell your God you don't trust His word? Should you keep telling yourself not to expect anything good? Words can give the adversary of your soul an opening to create havoc.

Faith and confession work together. As you study your Bible and speak the words of the Bible, you will build your faith. When faith grows, there is nothing that can stop God's power from manifesting itself.

Step one is to SHUT UP when it comes to negative expectations. Step two is to SPEAK OUT the promises and faithfulness of God.

The Bible places great emphasis on words. It says to "declare a thing and it will be established for you" (Job 22:28). God speaks precisely, and so should we. As we have done with our thoughts, we must also apply this first and most important test to our words: "If I speak this thing, will it help get me where I want to go? Do I want this thing I am speaking to actually happen?" For example, do you really want to speak against your marriage or utter a veiled insult, starting that argument with your spouse? When your words pass the test of "will they help or hurt me and those I love?" they are worth saying. **Remember that your words should agree with a kingdom purpose.**

Jesus said a most interesting thing in Mark 11:23: "For assuredly, I say to you, whoever says to this mountain, 'be removed and be cast into the sea,' and does not doubt in his heart, but believes that those things he says will be done, he will have whatever he says."

Jesus said to speak *to* the mountain, not to speak *about* the mountain. He said that if you speak to the mountain, and believe in your heart, then the mountain will be moved. We should indeed speak directly to our problems and the things that concern us by taking authority and dominion over them through the finished work of Jesus Christ. The Bible indicates that we have power, authority, and dominion on earth because of what Jesus did.

As the Bible tells us, the earth was created for Adam and Eve and their offspring. Adam and Eve lived in the Garden of Eden and were to live forever without pain, sickness, or death. When Adam and Eve sinned, their power, authority, and dominion over all the things of the earth were lost. They transferred authority and dominion over the earth to Satan. Jesus Christ won this dominion back for us by conquering sickness, sin, and death on the cross. 1 John 3:8 says: "He who sins is of the devil, for the devil has sinned from the beginning. For this purpose the Son of God was manifested, that He might destroy the works of the devil." We as children of God have dominion again. We need to use it.

Imagine a person living on a property with the wealth of an untapped oil well, never knowing it's there. Unlike that person, we must know that we have power, authority, and dominion over the things of this world, and over powers and principalities. These are exercised by speaking the Word of God in faith, freely using the name of Jesus, and pleading His blood, which has conquered all evil. The Bible tells us that many perish for lack of knowledge. We must know we have dominion over the negative influences in our lives, and we must use it.

Read the book of Ephesians, especially Chapters 1 through 3, to understand the power, authority, and dominion of the believer. New Age theology says that we can bring about whatever we seek by our own power. However, if what we seek is beyond our own power, and almost everything is, we need the power of God. We must speak in concert with the Word and will of God found in the Bible. Remember: The will of God is the Word of God.

As mentioned before, there are two kinds of "words from God." One is the *logos* word, which is written in Scripture quite clearly for everyone to see. The other is the *rhema* word, which is God's specific will for you given by the Holy Spirit in dreams, visions, circumstances, advice from others, or impressions and desires. The *logos* Word is always applicable; but it does not tell you what job to take, what spouse to marry, or any other specific thing. In order to know specifics from God, begin with the *logos* word and meditate on it. Next ask God for your specific instructions, if applicable. These will always also be scripturally linked. Then you can speak and act accordingly.

The experiences of our lives that shape our thought patterns also influence our words. We can use our words to overcome our thoughts and reshape our outlook. The Bible calls this the "renewing of your mind" (Romans 12:2). We can reprogram ourselves with God's Word and by refusing to speak words that lead to outcomes we do not want. We may have individual thought patterns that are hard to escape. Reprogram yourself with the Word of God on these issues and by properly employing thoughts and words.

As an exercise, you can assess your words. When you open your mouth, are the sentiments you express mostly random, neutral, critical, or negative? What comes out of your mouth when you are agitated? Being critical of others is a red flag. When you criticize others, you judge yourself. Your words are a window into your own soul. What bothers you in others may reveal how you see yourself. What you hate most in others may be what you hate most in yourself. This concept is developed a bit in Matthew 7 and Romans 2.

A negative spirit reveals a lack of trust and refusal to rest in what God has promised. Religion apart from grace and mercy can be hurtful and cause one to be critical of others. Since religious people, in themselves, cannot measure up to the difficult standards of the laws they put themselves under, they find much fault in others and are generally not pleasant to be around. Their lives reflect a lack of trust and refusal to rest in God's promises. How do you act and think when you are under pressure? This is what is in your heart and reflects what you truly believe about your life and circumstances. Most everything is, at its core, either fear-based or faith-based.

In order to move forward, stop engaging in idle speech. To help create a good future for yourself and your loved ones, make your words count. Do not spend time talking about other people or gossiping. Avoid wasting your time complaining. It would be much more useful to pray or be calm and quiet. Do an analysis of your speech, and it will reveal what is going on inside of you, inside your heart. Angry words may reveal fear; idle and wasted words may reveal a person without purpose or vision; and critical words reveal self-condemnation and fear.

Don't thwart the creative power that God gave you in your thoughts and words by allowing Satan to use his ideas to defeat you. Jesus utterly defeated Satan. Therefore, we have defeated him on every count. We are not helpless victims. If Satan troubles your mind, refuse to speak those things out loud. Do not verbalize your fears and worries. Instead, pray and speak the Scriptures against those outcomes. One of my favorites is Psalm 91 — a protection Psalm. I also like Isaiah 54:17, which says that no weapon formed against us can prosper. Christ conquered death, hell, and the grave. We are more than conquerors in Christ Jesus. We conquer by using words spoken in faith that agree with the Word of God. Why would you believe something that God Himself has said in the Bible, yet not believe there is power in those same words if you speak them? The Word of God works, no matter who speaks it.

Many situations in life are ambiguous. If you find you don't know what to say, the best advice is not to say anything. If you wish to receive anything from God, remember that thanksgiving and praise, not murmuring, are keys to victory. The Bible is replete with passages regarding the power of continually offering praise and thanksgiving to God. Make your words count and let that be your trademark. God spoke the world into existence. You are made in His image and likeness. What will you speak into existence? Words are seeds. You can use your words to build up and encourage yourself and others. You can use your biblically supported words to prophesy your future and improve your self-image and expectations.

Biblical Principles for Successful Living

You can use your words to improve every area of your life and the lives of those around you. They can be an encouragement to you and others. They can share wisdom from Scripture with those you are associated with. They can demonstrate faith. Perhaps, most importantly, you can use your words to lead others into an eternal relationship with God through Jesus. All of this can be done by speaking what God says in His Word. Use His promises as lights to guide and encourage your thoughts and words.

> **Proverbs 21:23:** "Whoever guards his mouth and tongue keeps his soul from troubles."
>
> **Proverbs 10:19:** "In the multitude of words sin is not lacking, but he who restrains his lips is wise."
>
> **Proverbs 25:11:** "A word fitly spoken is like apples of gold in settings of silver."

Pray this prayer over yourself and your loved ones each day out loud, as well as Psalm 91.

> **Numbers 6:24–27:** "The Lord bless you and keep you; The Lord make His face shine upon you, and be gracious to you; The Lord lift up His countenance upon you, and give you peace. So they shall put My name on the children of Israel, and I will bless them."

John began to realize that there were no excuses for less-than-desirable outcomes in his life. He realized that he could influence his future in large part though knowledge of the Word, prayer, and knowing and speaking God's promises. He began to tend to the garden of his mind, carefully weeding out repetitive, negative ideas and worries and replacing them with mental pictures of God's promises being fulfilled.

John realized he was in the blood line of Christ by faith, and that he was entitled to all the blessings listed in Scripture for accomplishing God's purposes. He removed the lies in his life he was believing and removed the mental crutches he tolerated that were enabling him to accept failure. He began to meditate on and quote Scripture out loud, which caused him to grow in faith. His verbal affirmations began to support his positive expectations. He began to think, speak, and act in a way that demonstrated an expectation of receiving the blessings of God, no matter what life threw at him. He slowly began to recognize God's voice by spending time listening in prayer.

Each morning he recited Numbers 6:24–27, Psalm 91, and several other verses out loud over his family.

John was excited to learn the truths regarding his words. He realized the negative and critical tones that he often expressed toward his wife and children were unwise at best and detrimental at worst. He realized that he should not speak things that he did not want to develop in his family or himself. When he felt worried or confused, he kept silent and prayed. He learned for the most part not to give voice to his fears. When he spoke, he spoke those things that built up and encouraged himself and others. And with his words, he began to reinforce his prayerful desires and vision for himself and his family. His faith began to increase.

Over time, John noticed that his positive expectation of answered prayer increased, his faith levels increased, his general attitude improved, and he even saw his prayers answered more often. His words no longer cast doubt on the faith which he professed in his Lord, nor worked against his desires, but rather propelled him forward. He was making God bigger and bigger in his life. He learned, when he was troubled, to be still and speak God's faithful promises against his worries and fears.

Chapter 8
Your Choices Show Who and What You Will Become

John 15:4–5: "Abide in Me, and I in you. As the branch cannot bear fruit of itself, unless it abides in the vine, neither can you, unless you abide in Me. I am the vine, you are the branches. He who abides in Me, and I in him, bears much fruit; for without Me you can do nothing."

Ephesians 5:7–9: "Therefore do not be partakers with them. Walk in light. For you were once darkness, but now you are light in the Lord. Walk as children of light (for the fruit of the Spirit is in all goodness, righteousness, and truth)."

John began to monitor his thoughts and use his words more wisely. He remained more positive and prayerful. However, he still spent several lunches a week with disgruntled co-workers and even occasionally went out with the guys for a few drinks after work. Occasionally — but especially when he was disappointed, sad, or lonely — he indulged in looking at provocative images on the computer. It initially gave him a rush of good feelings, but then he always came crashing back down to earth, feeling guilty that he had failed again to maintain the standards he aspired to as a Christian. When he felt guilty, he did not pray or fellowship nearly as much as he would have otherwise. He became very introspective. It was a bad cycle.

John expected that God would take away all of his wrong thoughts and desires after he became a Christian and believed that he should not have to exercise so much effort and self-discipline if he belonged to the Creator of the universe. "Wouldn't the temptations go away?" he wondered. Did the fact that he still struggled so often with the same old temptations indicate that he did not really know God? John wondered if he would always need to exert such seemingly enormous self-will to resist his undesirable, even sinful, tendencies.

Everyone makes hundreds of choices each day. Most are small and routine. Some are very significant. I heard an excellent sermon from Pastor Creflo Dollar years ago in which he pointed out that choices are the building blocks of destiny. Abiding in Christ involves making many good choices each day. Choices begin in the mind and end up in your actions. With one thought at a time, one word at a time, and one choice at a time, you sow and eventually reap your destiny.

Some of the most important choices you will make revolve around what relationships and associations you establish. Monitor your associations carefully. They generally predict or determine your future. Note what the Bible says on this subject:

1 Corinthians 15:33: "Do not be deceived: 'evil company corrupts good habits.'"

1 Corinthians 5:6b: "Do you not know that a little leaven leavens the whole lump?"

Proverbs 13:20: "He who walks with wise men will be wise, but the companion of fools will be destroyed."

Proverbs 27:10 (NIV): "As iron sharpens iron, so one person sharpens another."

It has been said that by looking at your friends, you look into your future. Choose your friends wisely. Close relationships and associations provide insight into who you are now — and a preview into who you will likely become. Friends can show you your weaknesses and strengths, and they can lead you into excellence or mediocrity. Be persistent in surrounding yourself with those who bring out the best in you and who represent who you want to become.

The same is true for mentors or people you admire and respect. Choose your mentors wisely. For example, do not try to learn how to be a millionaire from someone who cannot balance their checkbook. Find good mentors who have already successfully been where you want to go.

Another important choice concerns how you will spend your time. If you have a goal you wish to achieve, you would be wise to ensure that you are spending at least some time going in that direction each day. Make a small step each day toward this goal, and don't spend any time on activities that take you in the opposite direction. Many people wish for something but then make no effort to achieve it — or do counterproductive things that take them away from their goals. Remember these words, not definitively attributable to any one person but no doubt true: "The definition of insanity is doing the same thing over and over again and expecting a different result."

Your thoughts, words, and choices have gotten you to where you are today, and they will surely keep you there if you do not change something. Proverbs 4:7 tells us to seek wisdom. If you wish to accomplish something in life, increase your knowledge and wisdom in that area by seeking mentors, or by reading their books. You can gain many years of experience by reading a book written by someone who has achieved what you are aspiring to.

One mistake that many people do is to make a choice without thinking long term. If you're going to take a significant action or make a substantial change in your life, you should take time to envision the future ramifications of that choice in your mind. You should mentally strategize as if you were playing a game of chess: "If I do this, then this will happen; and if I do that, then that will happen." Choose your goals wisely. As many have said, "You don't want to climb the ladder only to find out it was against the wrong building."

If you are a parent, realize that children follow the examples they see. The power of example is enormous. It is especially important that you make good choices in the presence of the children you raise. Later in life, when confronted with a challenging situation, they will tend to do what they grew up seeing their parents do in similar situations. The most powerful initial influence on a child is normally a parent. Exodus 20:5 makes clear that the law of God causes the sins of the father to be visited upon the children to the third and fourth generations of those who hate Him. It's not God doing the visiting, but it can be the effect of the example. God will not punish children for the sins of their parents or vice versa. The example we see is the example we tend to follow. Always remember how important your example is and choose to set good examples for those you influence. And remember that when you make a wrong choice, you have a God of mercy, love, and grace to forgive you.

So what choices are you making every day? Are you exercising? Are you studying? Are you giving your time, talent, and treasure to good causes? Are you saving money each month? Are you sowing prayer, generosity, and kindness into other people? Do you purposely choose friends you want to be like? Do you date only those people you feel would be good marriage partners, or are you carelessly associating with people who might lead you the wrong way? Each day you are making choices that will yield corresponding results.

Genesis 8:22 reads, "While the earth remains, seedtime and harvest, cold and heat, winter and summer, and day and night shall not cease." In

Galatians 6:7–9, we learn that sowing and reaping is a law that will never change, which is built into the natural world and spiritual world: "Do not be deceived, God is not mocked; for whatever a man sows, that he will also reap. For he who sows to his flesh will of the flesh reap corruption, but he who sows to the Spirit will of the Spirit reap everlasting life. And let us not grow weary while doing good, for in due season we shall reap if we do not lose heart." Sowing specific actions reaps related results.

Another very important choice you will make relates to your money. An assessment of how you spend your money will reveal where your priorities are. Money is very important. Having money is not a sin. The *love of money*, however, is the root of all evil according to 1 Timothy 6:10. Money can be a false God-replacement, so be careful. The real power of money is in the opportunity to influence your life and the lives of others for the better. Maybe you can send someone to college or help the impoverished with food or housing through your generosity. The generous soul will be watered and blessed according to Proverbs 11:25. Let's look at some other Scripture verses that relate to money and giving:

> **Malachi 3:10–12:** "Bring all the tithes into the storehouse, that there may be food in my house, and try me now in this, says the Lord of hosts, if I will not open for you the windows of heaven and pour out for you such blessing that there will not be room enough to receive it. [11] And I will rebuke the devourer for your sakes, so that he will not destroy the fruit of your ground, nor shall the vine fail to bear fruit for you in the field, says the Lord of hosts; and all nations will call you blessed, for you will be a delightful land, says the Lord of hosts."

> **Proverbs 3:9–10:** "Honor the LORD with your possessions, and with the first fruits of all your increase; so your barns will be filled with plenty, and your vats will overflow with new wine."

> **Luke 6:38:** "Give, and it will be given to you: good measure, pressed down, shaken together, and running

over will be put into your bosom. For with the same measure that you use, it will be measured back to you."

2 Corinthians 9:6: "But this I say: He who sows sparingly will also reap sparingly, and he who sows bountifully will also reap bountifully."

Develop a giving lifestyle. While the New Testament mandate is to cheerfully give as your heart leads, keeping the motive of love foremost, a good yardstick to use in giving is the tithe. Seek to tithe or to give the first tenth of your income or increase, and be willing to give offerings beyond that. Tithing demonstrates God's pre-eminence in your life. It affirms that He has first place.

When you tithe and give offerings, God blesses you personally, materially, and spiritually. You can never out-give God. And while you should not give in order to get, it is highly likely that you will receive more from God than you give. Remember not to give grudgingly, for God's blessings come to those who serve and give lovingly, liberally, and cheerfully. If you are giving reluctantly, ask God to give you a greater willingness to give.

Guard your eyes and yours ears. Be aware that television can influence you the same way friends can. What we see in most television shows or movies can be contrary to the teachings of God. Most of these shows teach the value system of the world. Such values are opposite to the value system of God. Young children may grow up believing that the choices people make on television are acceptable. For example, if children routinely watch television shows where people freely engage in premarital or extramarital sex, they may well choose similarly if not taught otherwise by parents, church, or school. Much of what is routinely acceptable on television and in the movies these days is strictly forbidden by God in His Word.

Another common theme of television and movies is revenge. But God says to leave revenge to Him. It is wiser to use God's principles than any other principles you may have been taught or may encounter.

Be careful of extremes. Instead, choose moderation or balance. Sex is good within the confines of marriage, but it is not good before or outside marriage, or when it rules your life. A little wine may be good, depending on your persuasions; but wine or alcohol used excessively is detrimental, and drunkenness is a sin. Things can become idols in your life if you do not apply self-control. Even religion itself has been one of the greatest justifications for evil in the history of humankind — e.g., the Crusades, the Spanish Inquisition, and many radical or extremist religious groups or factions.

Patterns of evil have become so deeply entrenched in this world over the thousands of years since Eden that they are hardly recognizable as wrong anymore. What we consider normal today would have made people cringe twenty years ago. The only true source for the fulfillment of our needs — God — has grown dimmer and dimmer; while the false replacements, which at best incompletely satisfy our deepest needs, have grown louder and louder. They scream at us from television, movies, the Internet, social media, and every part of the world each day. We can only sit and wonder what has been programmed into us over the years and is influencing us subtly every day.

Prayer is critical, so make sure you do plenty of it. Make sure you pray for things with the right motive — to give God glory. And make sure always to give thanks in all things, as 1 Thessalonians 5:18 counsels. The importance of an attitude of thanksgiving and prayerful praise cannot be overemphasized.

You do not transform your life until you get your eyes off of yourself and onto God. Put God foremost in everything through prayer. Make sure you spend the necessary time waiting to hear from God. Most of our prayers are simply us talking to God about all the things we want. This contrasts sharply to the pattern the Apostle Paul followed in his many recorded prayers in Scripture.[18] He focused on the salvation of others, good citizenship, prayer for leaders, and the welfare of God's kingdom; whereas we tend to focus mostly on ourselves and our needs and desires.

Don't ever make critical decisions as a result of temporary situations or strong emotional feelings like fear or anger. And remember that you cannot consistently put yourself in dangerous or tempting situations and

---

[18] See Romans 1, 10, 12, 15; 1 Corinthians 1, 16; 2 Corinthians 1, 2, 9, 12, 13; Galatians 6; Ephesians 1, 3, 6; Philippians 1, 4; Colossians 1, 4; 1 Thessalonians 1, 2, 3, 5; 2 Thessalonians 1, 2, 3; 1 Timothy 1, 2; 2 Timothy 1, 4; Titus 3; Philemon.

expect to prevail. Although you may successfully avoid problems a time or two, you must keep yourself out of situations which could cause you to falter.

Remember that the only way to remain steadfast is to avoid tempting circumstances. If you wish to remain pure, don't put yourself in compromising situations with anyone who might lead you the wrong way. Do not abuse substances that impair your judgment or reduce your inhibitions. Do not allow pornography and sensuality into your mind. See Proverbs 4 on this subject, especially verses 14–15: "Do not enter the path of the wicked, and do not walk in the way of evil. Avoid it, do not travel on it; Turn away from it and pass on."

And do not remain isolated for too long — you need to be connected with others. The battle really is in the mind, and the battle is best won in the choices you make before the situation begins. Remember that you are not your own — you have been bought with a price (see 1 Corinthians 6:20).

Sin opens doors to guilt and condemnation and breaks all important focus. It also gives Satan opportunity to trouble you. For best results, follow Jesus as closely as you can. If you want peace of mind, then follow God's rules. Follow God's laws and avoid distracting stress, fear, worry, and doubt. If you do fail, immediately confess your sin and remember the grace of God so you are not fodder for condemning satanic activity.

You also have a choice as to what type of citizen you will be. The Bible says you should pray for your leaders, because God — and your votes — have allowed their appointment. Pray for them that you may live in peace and harmony. Pray for Presidents and their administrations, the Congress, and the judiciary. Pray especially for those individuals within these institutions we may think are far from God.

Additionally, the Bible tells us to pray for the peace of Jerusalem. Pray that our leaders and those in other countries of the world will follow God's plans and purposes, and will lead their countries in a way that is pleasing to God. Our job is always to pray for and support them. Freedom is worth standing for, and Christians should certainly vote and be involved in politics and other civic matters in a positive way.

Finally, remember this: You can teach someone what you know, but what you really are makes the biggest impact on those closest to you, who watch you daily. Make sure that you truly are what you say you are. If you make mistakes, confess and repent, and keep moving forward. A mistake or sin is what you did; it does not have to be who you are — or will always be.

One more point: Consistency is key. If you consistently do the right things, then you will achieve your desired results. Always be willing to admit your mistakes. Remember that it is easier to avoid trouble than to fix it after you are in it deeply. Try to avoid a problem or bad situation, whenever possible, *before* it has a chance to begin.

Chapter 9
A Few Random Pieces of Advice

Proverbs 4:23–27: "Keep your heart with all diligence, for out of it spring the issues of life. Put away from you a deceitful mouth and put perverse lips far from you. Let your eyes look straight ahead, and your eyelids look right before you. Ponder the path of your feet and let all your ways be established. Do not turn to the right or the left; remove your foot from evil."

Philippians 2:3–4: "Let nothing be done through selfish ambition or conceit, but in lowliness of mind let each esteem others better than himself. Let each of you look out not only for his own interests, but also for the interests of others."

This chapter offers bits of wisdom I did not put in other chapters regarding how to increase your chances of successfully navigating this life. The Bible makes clear that it's what you do for Christ that really counts — nothing else will last. The world is full of quips such as "You can't take it with you" and "You've never seen a U-Haul attached to the back of a hearse." The point is clear. Psalm 90:10 says we get seventy years or maybe eighty. What we do with those years has instant as well as eternal consequences.

Proverbs 19:23 tells us: "The fear of the Lord leads to life, and he who has it will abide in satisfaction; he will not be visited with evil." When you have life, you have the ability to influence the eternal. Looking at a dollar, we can see that it is a simple piece of paper or a computer entry. But if it is invested in a person's education, for example, then it can change a life and perhaps change the world forever. The words of encouragement that you say to people, the sharing of Christ with others, helping people with physical needs, and inspiring and rebuilding broken people are all opportunities that, if taken advantage of, will have eternal consequences for you and them.

    A truly successful life requires focus and determination. Life is a game of focus. Sin breaks focus. The many distractions of life in this world break focus. You must keep your focus to succeed. Some feel that if they belong to God and have the right motivation, things will work out without much effort. While it's true that God does sometimes miraculously intervene, we have to focus and apply the right principles, avoiding distractions, in order to achieve what we are called to achieve. Successful Christian living requires great effort as well as resting in what Christ has accomplished. That may seem like a paradox; but it means that Christians have been given the victory over Satan, yet are required to walk it out, utilizing scriptural principles, choosing to die to self, and letting Christ live through them.

    Proverbs 8 says to seek wisdom first (see verses 10–11). Proverbs 3:2 adds that if you keep God's commandments, length of days and peace will be added to you. Wisdom, of course, is the correct application of knowledge. Having knowledge is good, but having wisdom is better. In James 1:5, we have this promise: "If any of you lacks wisdom, let him ask of God, who gives to all liberally and without reproach, and it will be given to him."

    You need a big God, so seek to make God bigger and bigger in your life each day through proper focus. If you immerse yourself in soap operas, pornography, the news, or most television shows, God's influence on your life will diminish, and the things of the world will loom larger. Seek to magnify God in your life, and in doing so, you will magnify faith in your life. It is sad how people diminish what God has done in their lives. According to Romans 1:21, we should glorify God, and we should be thankful at all times. If we do so, we will magnify what God has done in our lives. Faith must be exercised like a muscle. Faith comes by hearing and hearing by the Word of God (see Romans 10:17). Therefore, read and meditate on the Word daily so that your faith will grow. Spend time in the presence of God. That is where you will find the victory resulting from faith in God's provision and promises.

Move forward and do not be chained to the past. If you have failed or made bad choices — or if you frequently hear the words "if only I had done this or that" in your heart and mind — then you are living with regret. Ask God to free you from these constraining agreements with the devil, or your prospects will in fact be self-limited. Learn to live without regret, shame, guilt, or fear. Regret, self-doubt, and fear cripple you. Peace and joy are decisions, and they require effort. In this world, there are many detractors and those who will come against you, so learn to be your own best friend. Look to the example of King David and others in the Bible, and encourage yourself despite your circumstances. Don't look to others for peace, joy, and affirmation. Look to God!

Fear is a debilitating emotion. If your life is affected by fear, deal with it. Partner with God to achieve His purpose — and then leave the results to Him. All fear is the fear of losing something you care about. Even if we do have things to lose, but are willing to give them up, there will be no fear. Doing what is right will protect you; but even when you do not do right, God may protect you, if you belong to Him and claim His promises. We read in 1 John 4:18 that perfect love casts out fear. So remember how much God loves you and that He is always watching over you and guiding you — and your fears will subside.

There can be a problem with some of the ideas and actions we often find attributed to God. For example, some might say that a loving God would never send anyone to hell. Of course, the standard Christian response to that would be that He does not send anyone to hell. We, in fact, send ourselves to hell by our choosing against Him. But would God allow some of His children to go to hell?

Another example might be that since there are many religions, all people of faith will be accepted by God, because a human father would never dismiss his child for his or her chosen beliefs. I do, however, want to say at this point that God will give everyone a fair chance.

Yet, while it is true that good, God-fearing fathers would love their children and would not want them to be hurt in any way, it is not true to say that no one can go to hell — or that all religions and behaviors are acceptable to God. God is God, and His exact nature is expressed in detail in Scripture. He must be defined and accepted by that standard and not some "common sense" standard that seems right to the average mind based on the ways of today's world.

It is clearly true that human fathers who honor God resemble God in many ways and that a loving God will do all He can to ensure all of His children will be with Him forever. We just need to work with Him and follow the divine plan. 2 Peter 3:9 tells us that God is "longsuffering toward us, not willing that any should perish but that all should come to repentance." God's wrath against sin has been poured out on Christ. His plan is that we must accept Christ as our sin-bearer, or we will face judgment.

Embrace the good that can come out of failure. Do not regret every negative circumstance or experience, or every enemy in your life. Friends normally give you affirmation and support, but enemies and tribulations stimulate your growth. While you should not unnecessarily antagonize an enemy, realize that it is through enemies, trials, and tribulations that you get the most growth. Enemies, challenges, and failures should be viewed as potential growth opportunities. Goliath certainly helped David. Pick your fights carefully, as there will be many to choose from. Focus on God, and joy will come. "Weeping may endure for the night, but joy comes in the morning" (Psalm 30:5b).

Don't sell yourself short. In the negotiations of life, set your sights high. If you are selling an item for a dollar, you may end up getting 50 cents. But if you're selling the very same item for $10, you may end up with $5. It's really that simple.

I am certainly not advocating engaging in unfair trade deals, but in many negotiations, you get what you expect and what you negotiate. Don't tell others how inadequate or untalented you are when in a job interview! Be your own biggest supporter. Look at the brighter side. Set your sights high up front. When you start high, you end higher.

Manage your expectations, and don't be deceived or disappointed when dealing with people. We know that people can change, especially when they come to know Jesus Christ as their Lord and Savior. But as a rule, you must remember a person is really best characterized by what they routinely do, not what they say. Unless you have a strong reason to believe otherwise, observe what a person has consistently done in the past and expect more of the same in the future.

Case in point: Don't marry someone, expecting to change them. It almost never happens.

Give much and expect nothing in return. When you give to God or others, you should derive your satisfaction from knowing you have done something that God approves of and blesses, not simply from the acknowledgement and response of others. If you do this, you will never be disappointed, regardless of whether your giving is appreciated or seemingly ignored. This is especially true in marriage. For best results, give without worrying about what you will get back. Do not keep record. Seek only to please God in your actions and judge yourself by that measure alone.

Define your personal goals very clearly. If you do so, you will be able to determine how you should react to life's situations. If someone asked you what characteristics you would most like to develop in your life, what would you say? Would you say courage, or boldness, or intelligence? Certainly those are worthy characteristics to develop. For me, the goal is to be more Christlike. The characteristics that are part of becoming more Christlike are many but would certainly include humility, patience, service to others, love of God and fellow man, and faithfulness.

When you face situations that at first glance appear to be defeats or negative events that diminish you, you should ask yourself if these situations are helping you develop those desired Christlike characteristics. If they are, then you should, as James 1:2 says, count those trials as joy because they are developing you into a mighty Christ-follower.

Plant the future harvest you desire. Sow good seed everywhere. Sow seed with your money; verbally prophesy the encouraging Word of God to yourself, family members, and others in faith; give your time, love, forgiveness, deeds of kindness, and acts of prayer and mercy freely. Whatever it is you need — more time, more energy, more money, more support, more relationships, more wisdom — just plant a seed by using what you already have. If you need more time, give more time to others. If you need more money, give money to someone who needs it. If you need more wisdom, share what wisdom you have with others. Give yourself away!

This is exactly the kind of attitude that God wants to bless and that will produce fruit in your life. You never know where the harvest will come from. God wanted a family, so He sowed His Son in death that He might reap many sons and daughters. God wants a willing, voluntary family, so He lets you choose Him. There can be no true friendship and no true relationship apart from choice. God gives us free will to choose to let Him plant the seed of salvation in our lives. Planting is an act of faith, and it brings glory to God. Use what you have now to get what you want or need.

Prepare for your moment of opportunity and be ready in advance to take advantage of the opportunities presented to you. This all goes along with establishing your goals and realizing your purpose and vision in life. Whatever your purpose and vision, be prepared for opportunities that may come along. Whether it is through the proper organization of a resume, or through reading and studying, or through making key associations and developing critical relationships — be prepared. Seek to be the very best in your chosen field. As Jesus' parable of the ten virgins illustrates, we must be prepared for opportunity so that we don't miss it.

I once heard Pastor T. D. Jakes preach an excellent sermon about tying our resources, family, and plans to God's purposes so that God will establish and protect them. Align your purposes with God's purpose. It is ultimately God's plan that He is most interested in achieving. Seek to fit into His plan and your efforts will be blessed accordingly. Make sure you understand your purpose, and make sure that it comes from God. A plan which originates from God and is tied to God's larger plan allows you to partner with God and obtain His support. Who will God support? He will most actively support the one who gives Him the glory and helps Him achieve His purposes on earth. What is His purpose? It is making disciples.

Be a person of integrity and keep your word so that people can trust you. Become servants of integrity. Choose to make the harder right decision over the easier wrong decision. Guard your principles. It is better to be poor than to steal and have to look over your shoulder for the police to eventually come. The Bible says that if you obey and respect authority, you need not fear anything from the government. See 1 Timothy 2:2 on this point. You will never need to fear the authorities if you are doing the right things and obeying the laws of the land. Always choose to do the things that will guard your integrity and principles and allow you to sleep well at night.

Use the 80/20 rule. Spend most of your time on what gives the most benefit. This principle is elaborated on in several books by Richard Koch. Assess what it is in your life or business that will give you the most positive results — probably you will find that only about 20% of your time is spent working on those items. It would be wise to spend at least 80% of your effort and time on the things which give you the most benefit.[19]

Take a personal inventory from time to time to see if your actions and attitudes are getting you to where you want to go. If you have lost sight of where you want to go, then immediately take time to determine it again. Consistency of behavior yields the best results.

A teachable person who is open to advice and counsel will go farthest, yet most people are not teachable. This is especially true for children with their parents. Make sure that you are teachable, and make sure that you learn from every person you meet. You never know who will give you God's wisdom. It might be coming from the person you would least expect to give it to you. Most people do not want to take wise advice but rather choose to make their own decisions. This is quite normal, but sometimes they end up learning life's lessons the hard way. It is better to avoid firsthand misery whenever possible.

There are a few keys to successfully getting along with others. First and foremost is putting the needs of others ahead of your own. This is especially true in marriage. Endeavor to see things from the other person's point of view. A secret to successful friendships is making other people feel better about themselves when they are with you, because you listen to or encourage them. People would rather be listened to by you, than to listen to you. People would rather tell you how much they know and have you praise them for it, than to hear how much you know, even though you may know a lot. Be a great listener, and people will automatically assess *you* as brilliant!

---

[19] Yaro Starak. What Is The 80/20 Rule And Why It Will Change Your Life. https://www.entrepreneurs-journey.com/397/80-20-rule-pareto-principle/. Also received permission from Richard Koch, The 80/20 Principle author.

The secret to successfully getting along with others begins with the realization that you are not the center of the universe. There are probably only a few people in this world who truly care very much about you, so don't expect too much from others. A good rule is to give much and expect little or nothing in return. With this in mind, when you give to someone, whether it be your children or your friends, give only the amount you're comfortable with. If you go beyond that, you may feel disappointed, resentful, and entitled to some payback when your recipient fails to show "proper appreciation." If you truly desire to give more, you can ask God to increase your loving capacity to give more without hesitation.

A quick word about the Internet: It is at once a blessing and a curse. Use it wisely. Do you know the purpose of the Internet? It is a commercial enterprise. Just like everything else, it is designed to make money. It has to be profitable, or it will not survive. Some of the big tech companies offer their products free but use the copious information they gather from everything you do to make money. That means that everything on the web is fair game for commerce and is available to many eyes. Any piece of data or personal history that anyone wants to buy can be sold to others and is limited only by a set of protective rules that are no doubt hard to enforce.

Retail companies, as well as Internet service providers may collect data on your buying, web-surfing, texting, and searching habits. These companies may then sell this information to other entities. That's why you may get notifications seeking to sell you things related to your browsing history or even words spoken on your phone. If there is a market demand for a type of information about you, then rest assured it will be supplied by the selling of your data if legally possible.

Your searches, emails, and texts are fair game. Do you want to land that great job, even run for political office some day? Companies may access the Internet or social media footprint you made as a teenager to determine your suitability. Take the long view when making your daily social media or Internet choices. Remember that God is always watching — that He is holding you accountable for everything you do — and that should cover it.

One last thought. It is my experience that God has made us so that we will not be truly happy unless we are sharing Christ or getting involved with others. A self-absorbed and inwardly-focused life will always lead to sadness and confusion. It is my admittedly medically uninformed belief that many suicides could be prevented if people would find a way to help others and focus outwardly. I have found that I am happiest when I am helping others. That is how God made us. The best kept secret to being happy in this life is serving others and being outwardly focused.

Chapter 10

How to Get Closer to God

2 Chronicles 16:9: "For the eyes of the Lord run to and fro throughout the whole earth, to show Himself strong on behalf of those whose heart is loyal to Him."

Upon introspection, John realized that the choices he was making in his associations and the example he was setting for his children and spouse could be better and were not moving him swiftly to his desired goals. His money management decisions were not going to help him achieve his financial goals, so he decided to employ God's principles in his finances. He worked to get out of debt, to give more money to his church, and to save more.

John also realized that he was wasting valuable time in the evening watching typical television shows and carelessly surfing the Internet. He began to pray and read the Bible with the kids. He listened more closely when his wife spoke to him — even in the middle of a ballgame on TV. He began to pray more. He listened to educational CDs on the way to work instead of just music on the radio. He even tried to exercise and eat healthier foods. He realized that he had to invest in and create his future by routinely making wiser choices on a daily basis.

There was no doubt that John's life was improving. He gained some mastery over his thoughts and speech patterns, and he was making better choices; but his relationship with God still seemed a bit distant and dry. It did not flow naturally. He continued to incessantly monitor his behavior, hoping to gain God's favor. He was up and down with his circumstances. He wondered what the key was to a more natural and consistently godly lifestyle. John wondered what it would be like to walk with God as "His friend," as Abraham and Moses had done. He wanted to feel closer to God. He knew emotions were not the most important thing. But he also knew something was missing. He did not really know how to pray naturally; and he wondered how to get closer to God, how to feel His presence, how to walk in His divine favor.

God must be pursued. A close and totally fulfilling relationship with Him will not be handed to you, even if you are a child of God by faith. There is a parable told about two dogs racing. Every Saturday a man would bring his two dogs into town to race. One dog was red, and the other was white. He would take bets on which dog would win. Some Saturdays the white dog would win, and some Saturdays the red dog would win; but the owner always bet correctly. People asked him how he always knew which dog would win. The man answered: "I mostly starve one and feed the other that week. The one I feed better always wins because he is stronger." Thankfully, this is a fictitious story, but it provides a good spiritual analogy.

This parable represents the conflict within us between our spiritual nature as Christians and our fleshly nature. The one that we feed is the one that will be dominant. The Bible talks about this age-old contest between the flesh and the spirit in Romans 7. How does one win the battle of the flesh versus the spirit? How does one walk by the Spirit rather than by the lust of the flesh, the lust of the eyes, and the boastful pride of life mentioned in 1 John 2:15–17? We win the battle and walk after the Spirit by making good choices and feeding our minds with biblical truth — while starving our minds of improper thoughts and ideas from the enemy.

Understanding and embracing God as the only source of all satisfaction, meaning, and purpose is critical to this life and to eternal life. He is the only source of living water. So many sins, so many distractions, and so many wrong choices result from people seeking to fulfill their inner needs in the wrong manner — or sooner than God has planned. What they fail to realize is that, ultimately, only God gives us full and lasting satisfaction in life. It is not found in many sexual partners, nor is it found in alcohol or drugs. Satisfaction is not found in activities of any sort, for they offer only temporary distraction. What we must realize,

Biblical Principles for Successful Living

embrace, and understand first and foremost is that the source of all true and eternal satisfaction is found only a deep and meaningful relationship with God.

Once you attain such a relationship with God, you will want to keep it. The salvation you gain by faith stays with you by faith — you don't need to perform works to keep it. If man could have attained salvation by the works of the Law, then Christ came to earth and died in vain. On this point, Paul reminds the Galatians (see 2:21) that they began their walk by faith and must continue by faith. He exhorts them to continue in faith and not revert to circumcision or other elements of the Law in order to stay saved.

We must constantly remind ourselves that the penalty for our sins — past, present, and future — has been paid. Our works did not save us, and they will not keep us saved. Nonetheless, the victorious Christian life requires that you spend time with God. You should choose to watch, hear, or read Christian TV shows, music, and books as often as possible. Spend time every day reading the Bible. Meditate on your bright future with wholesome thoughts and continue to make good choices. Grow toward the only One who can make you complete, because He is your Creator.

Remember that evil is so subtly intertwined in our world that it is often difficult to notice when wrong ideas work their way into our thoughts, words, and choices. Reading, journaling, praying, and enjoying God daily will make everything related to your faith much more real to you. A Christian essentially lives in another kingdom — even while here on earth. Therefore, here on earth, we are ambassadors of God's kingdom. We must make sure that we spend time with God in order for His principles and values to be alive and operative in us, and so that we are not overtaken by the corrupt principles and values of this world.

Since God has an enemy, we also have an enemy. That enemy is Satan, and his primary attack is on the mind. We may tend to think that our war is against people, but God's Word tells us in Ephesians 6 that our warfare is not against flesh and blood, but against spiritual powers and principalities. We are in a spiritual war.

Every day is an opportunity for spiritual combat for all of us who call ourselves Christians. But victory is ours, says the Lord. Ephesians

6:11–12 says to "put on the whole armor of God that you may be able to stand against the wiles of the devil. For we do not wrestle against flesh and blood, but against principalities, against powers, against the rulers of the darkness of this age, against spiritual hosts of wickedness in the heavenly places."

The challenge to choose to do the right thing for God and for your family is a daily challenge. One click on the computer may be all it takes to be exposed to all manner of evil things. Simply watching a typical television show may expose you to a parade of sexual innuendo, inappropriate sexual activity, irreverence, disobedience to parents, rebelliousness, theft, murder, and other negative and hurtful behaviors. We are in a war. We must keep our guard up and protect our hearts and minds as we prepare each day to "fight the good fight of faith" (1 Timothy 6:12).

Be prepared to fight each day, avoiding sin and compromise, and disciplining your body and mind. Where do strong people get their strength in tough times? It comes from growing deep, strong roots in God by spending time alone with Him in prayer and reading the Scriptures. The depth of authority and influence you have through Jesus Christ is directly related to the depth of your relationship with Jesus Christ. He is your Savior and source. The disciplines of the faith must be employed. The pursuit of God takes effort. Think of the persistent — and short — Zacchaeus, who climbed a tree to encounter Jesus, or of the men who let down their sick friend through the roof of a house where Jesus was so that this man could be healed. They would not take no for an answer.

A deep and meaningful relationship with God won't be automatic. Spend time in the Word. Spend time in fellowship and accountability. Talk to God as you would talk to a friend. Time, talent, and treasure invested in eternal things will yield eternal results. Leave a legacy. Pray for people — and never stop praying. Great things happen as a result of much prayer.

I read an interesting concept from Dr. Kenneth Hagin about a *fasted lifestyle* from his book *A Commonsense Guide to Fasting*. Besides the more traditional types of fasting, he also essentially suggested that a spirit-led lifestyle of some form of continual self-restraint was more useful than one long, painful fasting event.

Biblical Principles for Successful Living

To get closer to God, some like to occasionally fast from all food or perhaps certain types of food. Nowadays some do a media fast in which they avoid technology for a time. A person who does not consider it necessary to follow the dietary laws in the Scriptures might still routinely fast from pork or shellfish as a personal discipline.

Another method of fasting is to be in the habit of foregoing something in your life that you enjoy, either all the time or occasionally. My least favorite method of fasting is complete avoidance of all food. In the Old Testament, only The Day of Atonement, or Yom Kippur, required fasting from all food from sunset to sunset to focus on repentance (see Leviticus 23). Fasting with prayer for certain important results is frequently seen in such passages as Esther 4. In the New Testament, Jesus fasted for 40 days after His baptism and anointing, undergoing a testing period. A list of some fasting references in the Bible is found at this link.[20]

A person who is not spiritually diligent will find it difficult to stand strong and maintain great and satisfying faith. Everything worthwhile requires work — a good marriage, good job performance, good child-rearing, good anything. That's why, if you love what you do in your career, it is so much easier to apply full dedication. Pray for diligence and determination in your Christian walk. Choose to meditate on Scripture, not just read it. The devil cannot steal true God-given revelation from you. Revelation comes from meditating on the Word of God and spending time with Him. Work to get the true revelation of God's Word in your life.

Is God in control of this world or not? There are lots of opinions about this. I am personally persuaded that, yes, God is ultimately in control. But I am sure that He does not directly control everything that does or does not occur. God will only take charge of your life if you ask Him to. When you pray, that should be a main goal of your prayers. You will always see results from prayers offered in faith that claim a promise from God that you know you can count on as His will. After you pray for a certain matter, you should also begin thanking God that He has heard you.

Never stop praying. There is too much at stake. In Christ Jesus,

---

[20] Bible Verses about Fasting. https://www.biblestudytools.com/topical-verses/bible-verses-about-fasting/.

you have power and authority and dominion. God tells us in First Thessalonians 5:17 to "pray without ceasing." Jesus tells us that when we pray, we must believe that we will receive. In Matthew 21:22, we read: "Whatever things you ask in prayer, believing, you will receive."

In the Bible, the Sabbath was to be kept holy (see Leviticus 23). It was the seventh day. Keep a weekly Sabbath holy and devoted to God in some way. For example, you might avoid the things that give you pleasure in favor of helping others in some way, or simply focus primarily on God for the day. Be sure to rest. You might still attend church on either Saturday or Sunday. Practice the spiritual discipline of the Sabbath. The Sabbath was made for man, for the good of his body and the good of his soul and spirit. In Mark 2:27, Jesus says, "The Sabbath was made for man, and not man for the Sabbath." God instituted the Sabbath as a privilege and benefit, not a task and drudgery.

There is a great story I heard about two woodsmen — an old veteran and a young, strong newcomer. They decided to have a tree-cutting contest. The young man began chopping at the tree and did not stop. The older man stopped at least three times for short "breaks." But the older man who stopped for short breaks chopped his tree down first and won the contest. The younger woodsman was perplexed. After asking bystanders, he found out that, while the older woodsman was taking his breaks, he was actually sharpening his ax. The Sabbath is for resting from normal activities, sharpening our spiritual axes, focusing on and learning about God, pondering God's greatness, and building our faith. As our Creator rested on the seventh day, so should we set aside one day each week to rest from our labors. A weekly Sabbath is a great way to rest and to keep God first in your life.

Celebrating the annual biblical feasts in some way is also a really appropriate and fun thing to do for the Christian. The three major festivals every year — Passover (in Spring), Pentecost (in Summer), and Tabernacles (in Fall) — are actually comprised of seven times of celebration.[21] To fully keep each of the three major festivals would require a trip to Jerusalem and the new third temple (not there now). But to

---

[21] What Are the Different Jewish Festivals in the Bible? GotQuestions.org. https://gotquestions.org/Jewish-festivals.html.

Biblical Principles for Successful Living

acknowledge the festivals and be thankful to God for their fulfillment in Christ, both now and in the future, is a great opportunity for Jews and Christians to honor and obey God. You can give offerings or pay other forms of homage as a way to honor God at these (His special) times of the year.

None of these things will get you into heaven — that is the result of Jesus Christ having died for us on the cross to make us right with God by God-given grace through God-given faith. But it can be quite useful to routinely remind yourself, via fasting or some form of self-denial in humility and gratitude, whose you are.

Take time to minister to the Lord. Praise Him in the middle of pain and unpleasant circumstances. Paul tells us in 1 Thessalonians 5:18 to give thanks in all things, not necessarily for all things. To get to the next level, pray, praise, and give. Hebrews 11:6 tells us that "without faith it is impossible to please Him, for he who comes to God must believe that He is, and that He is a rewarder of those who diligently seek Him." Faith is essential. It is impossible to please God without faith. Pursue God and seek both His logos — written word — and His rhema word for your life's circumstances.

Giving to others is important. Isaiah 32:20 says, "Blessed are you who sow beside all waters, who send out freely the feet of the ox and the donkey." Acts 20:35 says: "I have shown you in every way, by laboring like this, that you must support the weak. And remember the words of the Lord Jesus, that He said, 'It is more blessed to give than to receive.'"

Follow hard after God. If you try, He will reward you many-fold. You simply cannot live in vital relationship with God without spending time with Him daily and practicing the spiritual disciplines that pay big spiritual dividends. When you fall in love with God, your life of faith will flow naturally, and obedience will be a pleasure. God does not play favorites. He will engage with you as deeply as you desire. He responds to you in proportion to your efforts to know Him better.

Don't be a lazy Christian. Walking with God is a blast! Don't forget that resting in what God has already done for you and claiming it by faith is a very important way to succeed. It is not all hard work and personal effort, but letting Christ live through you.

    John resolved to spend the first part of the day, just after waking, in a time of prayer and Bible reading, using a one-year daily Bible-reading plan. Some days he listened to an audio Bible on his phone as he sat quietly with his coffee and prayed. On other days, he sat in the presence of God and just listened, to see what God had to say to his spirit. John enjoyed going for long walks, listening to praise music and praying. His faith in God began to grow as he spent more time with his Maker. He began to love God more and more as he meditated on the love of God in Christ and his eternal salvation.

    John tried to remain cognizant of God at all times throughout the day. Soon he noticed his prayers flowing more naturally, powerfully, and with more emotion and power. He noticed God was becoming more real to Him, and sharing his faith became much easier. John also found himself becoming a mentor to many of his friends and his children on how to walk more closely with God. He realized he did not worry as much about life's challenges, because he sensed that God was always with him. His day-to-day fears and worries began to fade. He was becoming no longer afraid.

Chapter 11

The Most Important Concept Expanded Upon

John 15:20: "Remember the word that I said to you, 'A servant is not greater than his master.' If they persecuted me, they will also persecute you. If they kept my word, they will keep yours also."

James 1:12: "Blessed is the man who endures temptation; for when he has been approved, he will receive the crown of life which the Lord has promised to those who love Him."

Matthew 24:13: "But he who endures to the end shall be saved."

Psalm 34:19: "Many are the afflictions of the righteous, but the LORD delivers him out of them all."

John 16:33: "These things I have spoken to you, that in me you may have peace. In the world you will have tribulation; but be of good cheer, I have overcome the world."

Over the years, John experienced many very good and some very bad times. Several family members met an untimely death. This grieved him deeply. He felt God had let him down. As he grew older, he looked back on his own experiences and mentally reviewed the good times and favorable decisions, as well as the not-so-good ones. For example, once he left a job for another one simply because he became offended at being passed over for promotion. He felt he was not appreciated. That turned out to be a bad decision.

Several times John and his family left churches in search of the perfect one, which they never found. There were occasional marital difficulties and problems with the kids. John almost walked away from his Christian faith when bad things happened around the world that he could not understand or reconcile with his Christian faith. In the face of those difficult trials, feeling that God was far away, with no relief to be had, he sometimes wondered where God was — or if He really cared. Through it all, God held him closely. God never failed him, despite his emotional wanderings. Looking back, John was grateful.

> **Psalm 138:7:** "Though I walk in the midst of trouble, you will revive me; you will stretch out your hand against the wrath of my enemies, and your right hand will save me."

This book primarily emphasizes the positive aspects of the life of faith in Jesus Christ. It emphasizes the successful, happy, joyous Christian life, and that you can improve your chances of experiencing a meaningful and successful earthly life by following the principles found in the Bible. However, becoming a Christian will not ensure that you will avoid all trials and tribulations, the storms of life, or sometimes even gut-wrenching pain and suffering. These are common in the lives of all people, including Christians.

There are Christians all over the world who experience a very different reality than do the Christians in the United States. Some live in poverty or constant mortal danger, and many experience religious persecution of a brutal nature. For these reasons, this is probably the most important chapter in the book. We know there are good techniques and good habits that we should form and follow which increase our chances of a successful life. However, this earth is a spiritual battleground, so we have to become spiritual warriors.

Sometimes, despite best efforts, people get caught crosswise in the rubric of this fallen world. Some incidents are minor. Some are major.

Horrible things can happen to wonderful people, and it is usually not their fault. Within the last few years, as I have written these words, natural disasters, mass shootings, bombings, and many other acts of terror have occurred. It is imperative that we keep our guard up and continue to think, believe, speak, pray, and act correctly — and that we keep sowing good seed. We must never work against ourselves by careless speech or prayerlessness, and we must do everything we can to let God's power and protection flow. Expect and pray for the best. When something goes wrong, however, don't give up.

> **1 Peter 5:8–10:** "Be sober, be vigilant; because your adversary the devil walks about like a roaring lion, seeking whom he may devour. Resist him, steadfast in the faith, knowing that the same sufferings are experienced by your brotherhood in the world. But may the God of all grace, who called us to His eternal glory by Christ Jesus, after you have suffered a while, perfect, establish, strengthen, and settle you."

Things happen. You may find yourself in a minor fender-bender or in the middle of a Holocaust-like experience. You may find yourself accused unjustly, or as an unfortunate victim of a crime or a life-changing negative event. Someone you care about deeply will die, maybe even prematurely. In all the other countries in the world, there are millions upon millions of people who experience a much lower standard of living and generally much more misery than we do in the United States. Pain, suffering, and lack seem to be the norm for them.

I can only conclude that our fortunate position as Christians here in the United States is one from which we are to serve God and help others, fueled by Christ's love for the masses. We in the United States, and especially those of us in the middle- or upper-income levels, have been given exceedingly much compared to the rest of the world. As Christians, we are blessed so that we may be a blessing to others. We have been given a great deal in order to help others. Ephesians 2:10 says that God has prepared good works for each of us to accomplish.

In the book of Job, the faithfulness of Job and his love for God transcended his horrific pain and suffering. Job's devotion to God was eventually proven not to be based on the good things that God had done for him but, rather, on his relationship with God. He did not quit, even though he lost everything, and his wife even told him to "curse God and die" (Job 2:2). In the end, his righteousness and continued obedience were shown to be based on his relationship to and love for God alone. Thus, Satan's ploy to turn Job against God by causing negative events was defeated.

The harsh criticisms by Job's friends were also incorrect. Their criticisms represented typical religious thought, which says that suffering and pain are always a result of sin or personal guilt, and that if you are a righteous person, you should never experience such pain. This was and is patently false. Do not believe that lie, and do not become discouraged on top of your other sufferings should they occur. Remember that God's death penalty for sin has been paid by the blood of His own Son, Jesus Christ.

Throughout history, individuals and groups of people have faced difficult circumstances through which they demonstrated to all, just as Job did, that their love for and devotion to God were not merely a result of good fortune or the hope of His blessings. Every one of us also will have this opportunity to remain faithful in the face of sadness in our lives. Our faith must be strong, not only in times of blessing but also in the face of pain and sadness.

God and Satan are in a war for the souls of men and women. We do not always know the boundaries that God will allow Satan; but God is God, and He will someday reveal the wisdom of His plans to us. Never question God's motives. He has promised that He will make all things right in the end. So once again, while you are blessed and while you have much provision, use it in covenant with God to bless those around you and be His hands and feet. Expect and believe for the very best results, claiming the promises of Scripture for protection and healing and provision, frequently saying them aloud. If suffering should befall you, show your relationship with God to be real, thereby crushing the head of Satan and honoring God in your obedience. You will forever be glad you did.

In the United States, we have one of the highest standards of living in the world. If we have food on the table, money in the bank, clothes to wear, and a job, then it is said that we are in the top few percent of the world's population. But still, many people, even in the United States, feel much pain and sorrow daily. Any of us could be one breath away from having our lives turned upside down. Unmet expectations or great disappointments can be very difficult — especially if we have been taught that once we become Christians, our problems are over. Many Christians set themselves up for despair by thinking that when they are saved, they will experience only the good life. We must use good principles, such as praying for protection and claiming God's promises aloud, as well as others we have discussed throughout this book, and we must never quit on God when something goes awry. As Peter said to Jesus: "Lord, to whom shall we go? You have the words of eternal life" (John 6:68).

God is not a vending machine who only dispenses His blessings to us. As mentioned several times before, God has an enemy, and so do we. The enemy must be resisted by using the principles outlined in Scripture and this book. You should obey the Word, speak the Word, and cover yourself and your loved ones in constant prayer, expecting God's protection and favor. If we get caught up in the negative side of the great spiritual tapestry which exists all around us, we must remember that Jesus is there to help, guide, comfort, and, above all, give us eternal life. Only after this life will we be rid of all pain, suffering, and misery. While we have life and blessings, let us serve God with all of our hearts. We should give our time and treasure to the sick, poor, orphans, widows, and prisoners. We should pray for that which we are to achieve on His behalf. In doing so, we store up treasure in heaven.

When something bad happens, regroup and recover. Then resume the attack. You can use good principles, you can think right, you can speak right, and you can live right; but there are still things in life that may go wrong and that you will not understand. When bad things happen, remember that you signed on with God so that you could be forgiven of your sins and go to heaven when you die. Remember that God said He would never leave you or forsake you (see Hebrews 13:5). Remember also that most of your growth occurs in the times of trial. Do not waste your time of pain, but seek to determine what you can learn from it if at all possible.

Accomplishing God's purpose is not a contest. Beware that you don't seek to outperform other Christians or cast your greatness in God's sight by what you can achieve on His behalf. The highest and best rewards in the Kingdom of God come to those who humbly do what God calls them to do, using however little or much they have, with the proper motive, which is the love of God. A mother faithfully raising her children may not feel very significant, but she is sure to enjoy the same reward from God that a great evangelist might receive when she arrives in heaven. This is because they both answered God's call and accomplished the mission they were called to achieve.

Do what you are called to do by aligning yourself with God and accomplishing your purpose. Don't be discouraged by comparison. While you still have life, you have a purpose to accomplish if you are a Christian. You should expect Him to meet your needs and help provide for the fulfillment of His vision for your life and your part in His kingdom.

Do not let the past dictate your future. Never quit because of pain, sadness, defeat, or failure. You cannot lose if you will not quit. Philippians 3:13–14 encourages us: "Brethren, I do not count myself to have apprehended; but one thing I do, forgetting those things which are behind and reaching forward to those things which are ahead, I press toward the goal for the prize of the upward call of God in Christ Jesus."

Don't doubt God. He never promised a smooth ride. Life with God is exciting and full of wonderful revelations and experiences. However, God did not promise that there would always be smooth sailing. Look at those mentioned in the faith Hall of Fame found in Hebrews 11. Some of these individuals were exalted beyond measure in this world, while others were tortured and martyred.

Note that Jesus died at the height of His ministry, in His early thirties. He had fulfilled His divine purpose. The apostle Paul said, "For to me, to live is Christ and to die is gain" (Philippians 1:21). Understand that pain and suffering are normal parts of life, and they usually promote growth. Growth is necessary to fulfill your purpose. Every experience can teach us something, and we must ensure that it does. Even death itself will come to everyone, but it is just the gateway to eternal life and ultimately is gain for the Christian. If you are a child of God, then you should welcome death when the time comes.

Biblical Principles for Successful Living

Why do you grieve if you lose money? You cannot take it with you. God promises His children that He will provide for them. King David said that he never saw the righteous person forsaken or his seed begging for bread (see Psalm 37:25). Bad things can shake your vision and sense of purpose. Get right back on track. Sin or negative events can get you off track. He who endures to the end shall be saved and shall accomplish His purpose. Don't let Satan steal your vision, purpose, or faith. When things go wrong, do not assume that they are going to go all the way wrong, causing you to give up. Rather, keep on praying and expecting the next good thing from the hand of God.

Learn to be patient when you do not understand things. Learn to accept the dichotomies of life that you cannot reconcile and don't let them throw you off track. Give them over to God every day. Don't liken or compare your own experiences and choices to the experiences and choices of others. Deal with the reality God gave you — and no one else's reality. In other words, don't judge God by all the sad events happening around you involving other people. God has told us that in a man's life, there will be many days of darkness (see Ecclesiastes 11:8). He also counsels us that "many are the afflictions of the righteous, but the Lord delivers him out of them all" (Psalm 34:19).

Stay in your lane and thank God often for His tender mercies. When you find yourself experiencing "weaknesses, insults, hardships, persecutions, and calamities" (2 Corinthians 12:10), something strange isn't happening to you (see 1 Peter 4:12). Jesus suffered these same things, and it is what we must expect as we sojourn through this world. So, if something bad happens, let's not ask, "Why me?" but instead, "Why *not* me?"

Do not avoid becoming a Christian or consider leaving the faith because you sense hypocrisy among believers or because you can't understand the bad things that happen to other people. "[God] makes His sun rise on the evil and on the good and sends rain on the just and on the unjust" (Matthew 5:45b).

Is God sovereign? Yes! The outcome of the game of life depends in part on the efforts the players exert. It is much the same for Christians. Results depend on faith, knowledge, and wisdom gained from seeking God, as well as efforts expended and prayers prayed. God is certainly sovereign over the big picture. Although it is clear that He is not controlling all individual events, God does ensure "that all things work together for good to those who love God, to those who are the called according to His purpose" (Romans 8:28). And He is there to stand with us when the pain is too great to bear.

The Bible also says that God orders the steps of the good man (Psalm 37:23). Those who would be successful Christians must call upon the finished work of Christ for victory and the power of God to do good works and prevail. Your prayers should invite God to bring about His will in your life. God wants a relationship with you. Remember, this is the most important relationship you will ever have.

It would be difficult to describe all the painful realities that people have faced throughout history. Many have experienced unspeakable horrors. Many have lost children and loved ones prematurely. Some have seen war and death and sadness on an ongoing basis. Some have never known a home or a family's love. These people's experiences are products of a world infiltrated by Satan. God has given man free choice; but man has too often chosen to use it very badly, and he has hurt many others in the process.

God loves to turn deaths into resurrections and bring triumph from trouble. He wants to use that problem, hardship, or pain to bring some good into your life whenever possible. 2 Corinthians 4:16–17 says: [16] "Therefore we do not lose heart. Even though our outward man is perishing, yet the inward man is being renewed day by day. [17] For our light affliction, which is but for a moment, is working for us a far more exceeding and eternal weight of glory."

For those who have experienced great pain, loss, and failure, the Bible offers encouragement. Your pain won't last forever. God exhorts you to continue on. For what choice have we but to begin again each day, either with or without God. Follow the principles of the Holy Scriptures and press forward in greater anticipation of blessings and victory in the future. Sow your seeds of pain for a harvest of present and eternal blessings. When Jesus asked His disciples if they, too, would leave Him, Peter answered and said: "Lord, to whom shall we go? You have the words of eternal life" (John 6:68). Surely our answer is the same: To whom else would we go? God has told us in His Word that if we call upon Him, He will be with us. He will act on our behalf, and He will involve Himself in our lives. So just keep going.

God has also told us that if we put our trust in Him, then we will be with Him forever. If you have experienced pain, do not blame yourself in any way. The world we live in is so full of evil that it is only by God's grace that we ever escape. No doubt we have escaped far more often than we realize. In this world there will be trouble (see John 16:33), but we should not fear, because God is with us and will never leave us. Be of good cheer, for God has overcome the world. Go forward and don't quit, for eternity will bring you much joy.

Break the chain of worry. The vast majority of the things we fear never come to pass. Many people forge a chain of worry. It goes something like this: You might envision yourself losing your job. If you lose your job, you might lose your house. If you lose your house, you will have to live on the street until you die from starvation. Normally, even the first thing in the worry chain doesn't happen. But even if the worst happens, you needn't fear. Once you do not fear death, you do not need to fear anything — and if you know Christ, you need not fear death.

God cannot be put in a box. He will never be totally predictable, but He gives general guidelines and principles about Himself in Scripture. Sign up with God for the right reasons — for salvation, not for a joyride or a life without any troubles. Be careful to understand what faith is and what God promises. Remember: God truly loves you, so just love Him back. Do this by spending time with Him, praising and thanking Him. You will be surprised at the results.

Note: The information in this paragraph is my personal thought, which is not necessarily from Scripture. You might ask God for a special arrangement, e.g., that when times are tough, He will show you something in particular that is special to you — a rainbow, a red bird, a dragonfly, a penny on the street, or a certain time on the clock. You can agree with Him that whenever He shows that special thing to you, it will assure you that God loves you and He is with you. Very often these signs will show up and you will find encouragement just when you need it most. We should not seek a sign to believe in Him (see Matthew 16:4), but we can always leave the door open for encouragement. Consider it a touch from God. Thank the Lord and feel His love. But even when you do not feel Him, you can know that He is with you.

The story is told about the boy who helped a butterfly out of a cocoon.

He helped the butterfly to escape prematurely, before the butterfly was really ready to be released and fly. As a result, the butterfly did not thrive, because it did not get a chance to develop and strengthen its wings during the process of removing itself from the cocoon. Likewise, if we are rescued from too many things, or if we are rescued prematurely, we may never get a chance to develop the skills we need for this life and eternity.

For example, if a person decides to give a church all the money it needs to build its new building, the church leaders and congregation might never develop the faith required in reaching out to the community and seeing God work. The members of the congregation might not have the opportunity to be blessed through contributing, and prayer would be diminished. We should not seek to remove minor stresses too quickly from ourselves or those we love. Sometimes our idea of blessing someone ends up preventing what God is truly trying to do with a person's life, because we rescued them from a potential growth experience too early.

Times of trial and difficulty are a double-edged sword. They are often painful and difficult, but they are also responsible for most of our growth as mature Christians. James 1:2–4 says: "My brethren, count it all joy when you fall into various trials, knowing that the testing of your faith produces patience. But let patience have its perfect work, that you may be perfect and complete, lacking nothing."

I remember hearing a sermon many years ago from Bishop Kenneth Ulmer in which he spoke of one of King David's methods for encouraging himself. In Psalm 18:1–3 we find David's keys to overcoming negative circumstances. In verse 1 the Psalmist says, "I will love you, oh Lord, my strength." So, loving the Lord is step one. Verse 2 says, "I will trust you." Trusting the Lord is step two. Verse 3 says, "I will call upon the Lord." Calling upon the Lord is step three. Verse 3 closes with this statement: "So shall I be saved from mine enemies."

Love the Lord, trust the Lord, call upon the Lord. So shall you be saved from your enemies. Never give up.

Looking back, John concluded that most of his best decisions in life were a result of deciding not to become offended and to stay the course. When painful situations arose, he kept the faith and praised God for all the good times. John concluded that the key to victory in life is to never quit as a result of getting angry or offended, or experiencing pain or loss. He learned that the best approach is to trust God and never stop employing the right principles. Just keep going, no matter what. "What else is there to do anyway?" he thought.

Chapter 12
Why Feelings and Fears Must Not Be Your Guides

Proverbs 3:5–6: "Trust in the Lord with all your heart and lean not on your own understanding; in all your ways acknowledge Him, and He shall direct your paths."

Romans 1:17: "For in it the righteousness of God is revealed from faith to faith; as it is written, 'The just shall live by faith.'"

2 Timothy 1:7: "For God has not given us a spirit of fear, but of power and of love and of a sound mind."

Proverbs 29:25: "The fear of man brings a snare, but whoever trusts in the Lord shall be safe."

1 John 4:18–19: "There is no fear in love; but perfect love casts out fear, because fear involves torment. But he who fears has not been made perfect in love. We love Him because He first loved us."

Hebrews 10:38–39: "Now the just shall live by faith; but if anyone draws back, my soul has no pleasure in him. But we are not of those who draw back to perdition, but of those who believe to the saving of the soul."

John noticed that, while he was generally living a more victorious life, his faith really "felt" stronger when things were going well — and weaker when he faced difficulties. He was "up" when things were "up" and "down" when things went wrong. He was strongly influenced by people, events, and circumstances. He was a man of powerful, enthusiastic prayer when everything was going as he desired; but he worried, doubted, and struggled to pray when things went wrong. His faith was up and down, almost always in direct response to events in his life that impacted his emotions and feelings.

John also was afraid of losing the things he cared about — like his job or his children or his money. His deepest belief was that if all was going well, God loved him and was pleased with his behavior, and that he had an "open heaven" because he was being obedient. But if things went badly, he could not shake the feeling that he was not pleasing to God and that he was doing something wrong. He wondered what spiritual principle he could learn that would enable him to be a more consistent person of power in the Lord, even when the chips were down.

If you trust your senses to verify what you should believe, Satan will defeat you. Instead, walk by faith in the unchangeable truth of the Word, and you will be spiritually invincible. Walk by faith and not by sight (see 2 Corinthians 5:7). Remove from your life the condemnation, fear, and shame that come as a result of past actions or failures; and accept grace, which leads to righteousness.

The book of Titus teaches us that we are being trained for righteousness by the very same grace that saved us. "For the grace of God that brings salvation has appeared to all men, teaching us that, denying ungodliness and worldly lusts, we should live soberly, righteously, and godly in the present age, looking for the blessed hope and glorious appearing of our great God and Savior Jesus Christ" (Titus 2:11–13).

Remember that you are the righteousness of God in Christ. You are entitled as a child of God to all the best that God has to offer through Christ. Get rid of self-focus and sin-focus. Christ came to free us from the worry and guilt associated with sin. Since our sins are forgiven — past, present, and future — we are free as Christians to focus outside of ourselves and be an instrument of God's love in this world. The blood of Christ continually cleanses us of all unrighteousness, and we are sealed for eternity by His Spirit.

Do not build up the false expectation that you will have no troubles in this life. Yet, do not be afraid to expect good things from God. Why are people afraid to give it all they have? It is because unmet expectations are very painful. Do not fear the future, but rather boldly expect God's best. Believe above all that God's plan will be accomplished in your life, even if things do not look rosy. Philippians 1:6 says: "Being confident of this very thing, that He who has begun a good work in you will complete it until the day of Jesus Christ." You must be fully persuaded by the Word of God rather than your experiences.

> **Hebrews 11:1–2:** "Now faith is the substance of things hoped for, the evidence of things not seen. For by it the elders obtained a good testimony." John 15:7 says, "If you abide in me, and my words abide in you, you will ask what you desire, and it shall be done for you."

How do you become fully persuaded? Romans 10:17 tells us, "Faith comes by hearing and hearing by the Word of God." But merely hearing the Word of God is not enough. Meditate on and speak the Word of God until it becomes real to you. This builds all-important faith, and without faith it is impossible to please God (see Hebrews 11:6). Remember also that God is no respecter of persons, as the Apostle Peter states in Acts 10:34. What He will do for one, He will do for another. He will do it for you as you believe. God loves to be trusted, and He honors people's faith in Him and His love for them. It's similar to how a parent feels when their child jumps into their arms, knowing that the parent will safely catch them.

Righteousness has always been by faith. Abraham was made righteous and was reconciled to God by faith well before the Law was ever given, and certainly well before Christ came to earth as Messiah. This is called the Abrahamic Covenant. God responds to faith in Him and His provision of grace much more than anything else. Since it is impossible to please God without faith, take every opportunity to build your faith through reading and meditating on the Word.

When someone asks if you are going to heaven, you should say, "Absolutely!" People may look at you as if to say: "But how can you know that? Isn't that arrogant on your part?" Well, how can you know you are saved? It's not because you feel that way, or because you are behaving well at the moment — it's because God said it. You can be sure of it because your trust is in God, and not in your own inconsistent behavior. You can check yourself to see if you are in the faith; but if you have sincerely asked the Lord to be your Savior, you should never doubt again, no matter how you feel.

God is always rock steady, even when we are tossed about by the storms of life. The Gospels tell of us a night when the disciples and Jesus were in a boat, and the sea became so stormy that the disciples feared for their lives (see Matthew 8:23–27). Yet, Jesus was sleeping peacefully. When the disciples awoke Jesus, He said to the storm, "Peace, be still!" It worked! Jesus is Lord over the storm, and He does not change. God does not change, despite how you may be pushed back and forth by life's events. "Jesus Christ is the same yesterday, today, and forever" (Hebrews 13:8).

There are many things in life that may trouble you if you focus on them. Give your unresolved issues and unanswered questions to God. That is the evidence of faith. If issues or life circumstances arise that you cannot understand or answer, "Do not be afraid; only believe" (Mark 5:36) — or, "Do not be afraid; only keep on believing [in Me and my power]" (Amplified Version).

Erratic behavior comes from being ruled by your emotions. Never make important decisions when you are emotionally stressed, hurt, angry, tired, or offended. Just waiting a few hours or giving it a night to sleep on the decision will prevent you from making impulsive decisions that you might regret later.

Be wary of getting offended in relationships. Robert L. Deffinbaugh points out that even John the Baptist, during the worst moment of his life, the day of his beheading, became unhappy with Jesus and felt offended by him. This is understandable, given his human frame and his imminent execution. He sent a message to Jesus through his disciples from prison: "Are you the Messiah, or should we look for another?"

This confusion was coming from John the Baptist, the same man who had identified Jesus as the Messiah and seen the Holy Spirit descending on Jesus after he had baptized Jesus for all to see. John told people that the Messiah would come with power to conquer, and he thought it was time

Biblical Principles for Successful Living

for Jesus to act accordingly — to do as he had said the Messiah would do. John was focused on the judgment side of the Messiah's coming, but Jesus was focused on the salvation side. It was His first coming. He will come again, riding the white horse of the conquering King.

Jesus' response to John was very simple: "Jesus answered and said to them, 'Go and tell John the things you have seen and heard: that the blind see, the lame walk, the lepers are cleansed, the deaf hear, the dead are raised, the poor have the gospel preached to them. And blessed is he who is not offended because of Me'" (Luke 7:22–23).[22] God is about God's plan and God's business — and we need to line up and give Him all the glory. He must increase, while we decrease.

A very wretched and effective demonic spirit is the spirit of fear. It manifests itself in many ways, including anger. Do not act under the direct or indirect influence of fear. Several hundred times in the Bible we find verses telling us not to fear. In fact, it is a command. It is absolutely essential that we do not fear. Some of the worst decisions in life are the result of fearing what might happen if we take a chance, or fearing rejection, failure, or disappointment — to the point where we don't take healthy risks and thereby miss opportunities. Some manifestations of fear are anger, depression, stress, and emotional fatigue. Fear is a killer of joy, creativity, and appropriate risk-taking.

Revelation 21:8 warns us: "But the cowardly, unbelieving, abominable, murderers, sexually immoral, sorcerers, idolaters, and all liars shall have their part in the lake which burns with fire and brimstone, which is the second death." Notice that the Word mentions the cowardly and fearful. God considers cowardice and fear great sins because faith is fundamental to the Christian's walk. We must trust in Him. He wants us to trust in Him.

Fear takes territory from you and pushes you into a smaller area of influence by restricting your activities and hampering mental engagement. It is impossible for the average person never to feel fear, but you must deal firmly with it. It is a faith-killer and victory-killer. If you would like to minimize all fear in your life, the safest place to be is in the will of God.

---

[22] Deffinbaugh, Robert L. 22. "John's Problem with Jesus" (Luke 7:18-35). Bible.org. https://bible.org/seriespage/johns-problem-jesus-luke-718-35.

Make choices that keep you in the will of God. People who obey God and the laws of the land have no basis for fear. When one is solidly in the will of God, there is no need to fear.

Remember that for God to operate in your life, He needs you to have faith. For Satan to operate in your life, he needs you to have, among other things, fear. Faith and fear cannot exist together. The Christian's faith is anchored in God's love. Fear, simply stated, is unbelief or weak belief. As unbelief gains the upper hand in our thoughts, fear takes hold of our emotions. Our deliverance from fear and worry is based on faith, which is the very opposite of unbelief. Make sure that you are squarely in the will of God and that you know your purpose; then give it all you've got and don't hold back. Don't be afraid to fail. Failure is often the best teacher.

Remember one more very important thing about fear: God, in fact, commands us not to fear. How many of us enjoy disobeying a command of God? No one, we hope! **We are COMMANDED not to fear.** "Have I not commanded you? Be strong and of good courage; do not be afraid, nor be dismayed, for the LORD your God is with you wherever you go" (Joshua 1:9). God's commandment not to fear is repeated throughout the Scriptures.[23] Do an Internet search on fear verses in the Old and New Testaments. God clearly commands us that we are not to fear.

God is more interested in our spiritual development than in our comfort. Expect to learn a lot when you are in God's plan, even from the negative events. Stay focused and be diligent. Never forget to pray, and don't forget to ask God for what you need. The asker has a much greater chance of receiving, so ask big. God says in James 4:2–3: "You lust and do not have. You murder and covet and cannot obtain. You fight and war. Yet you do not have because you do not ask. You ask and do not receive, because you ask amiss, that you may spend it on your pleasures."

Expect good things to take time. As the Scripture says, "For who has despised the day of small things?" (Zechariah 4:10). There are large species of trees that grow downward for several years, establishing strong, deep roots before they begin to show substantial upward growth. This appears to be a picture of the way the great people in the Bible were trained

---

[23] See, for example, Isaiah 41:10; Jeremiah 1:8; Deuteronomy 31:6; Luke 12:32; and Mark 5:36.

and forced to wait under difficult circumstances before receiving their ministry. People such as Abraham, David, Moses, Joseph, and Paul all waited long periods of time from the promises of God to the manifestation of great ministries.

Do not allow your circumstances or feelings to affect your conviction of God's presence, and that He is a good God who loves you dearly. The story of Joseph is found from Genesis 30 through Exodus 1. How do you think Joseph felt when he was imprisoned after Potiphar's wife had falsely accused him of attempted rape? His faithfulness eventually led to his release from prison and Pharaoh's subsequent elevation of him to number two leader in Egypt, second only to Pharaoh himself.

Believe what the Bible says — believe that God, His Word, and His promises never change. Real biblical faith is faith in God's love for you and in all the promises in the Word of God, no matter what you are experiencing. If you do not believe God loves you, then you will never be able to really trust Him. If you don't trust Him, you won't live for Him. Don't live by feelings, or even exclusively by facts. Live by biblical truth and faith in the Word of God.

> **Philippians 1:27–28:** "Only let your conduct be worthy of the gospel of Christ, so that whether I come and see you or am absent, I may hear of your affairs, that you stand fast in one spirit, with one mind striving together for the faith of the gospel, and not in any way terrified by your adversaries, which is to them a proof of perdition, but to you of salvation, and that from God."

> **Luke 1:74–75:** "To grant us that we, being delivered from the hand of our enemies, might serve Him without fear, in holiness and righteousness before Him all the days of our life."

William Lake

Chapter 13

Things to Know About Marriage and Relationships

Proverbs 31:10: "Who can find a virtuous wife? For her worth is far above rubies."

1 Corinthians 13:4-8, 13: "Love suffers long and is kind; love does not envy; love does not parade itself, is not puffed up; does not behave rudely, does not seek its own, is not provoked, thinks no evil; does not rejoice in iniquity, but rejoices in the truth; bears all things, believes all things, hopes all things, endures all things. Love never fails. But whether there are prophecies, they will fail; whether there are tongues, they will cease; whether there is knowledge, it will vanish away. And now abide faith, hope, love, these three; but the greatest of these is love."

After your decision to trust Christ as your Savior, the single most important decision you will make in life is the choice of your life partner. The ideal for scriptural marriage is one man and one woman — for life. As the years pass, they bond together and become one flesh. They help each other in life, bear each other's burdens, and become very comfortable in each other's presence. Marriage should get sweeter as the years pass and memories grow. This, however, is not realized in all cases, and young people considering marriage would do well to understand the importance to God of marriage and choose as wisely as possible with eyes wide open and the firm resolve to stay the course.

Typically, a young man will find a young lady he is greatly attracted to, and he simply "knows" in his heart that he could spend the rest of his life — *just looking at her*. This period of intense attraction normally lasts about two years. Then the realities of being with another person for life begin. The continuing feelings of normal attraction will be based upon many factors other than appearance. The man and the woman must learn to respect, admire, and appreciate each other for a strong marriage bond to develop and last. They must build a life together, pulling the marital rope in the same direction, and they must help each other to achieve God's purposes for their lives. Choose wisely and be determined to do what it takes to grow together.

John continued to get stronger and stronger in the faith. He was noticed as a man of God at his place of work. People often confided in him and asked his advice. One day a friend — let's call him Jim — asked John some questions about marriage. After Jim and his first spouse divorced, he married again. He was experiencing some of the same issues with his second wife that he had experienced with his first wife. Also, the pastors and teachers Jim encountered on TV, the web, or in person all had varying opinions about the state of Jim's soul. On top of that, as a result of the divorce, one of Jim's children drifted away from him a bit. There were issues with the blended family in his second marriage — such as how to discipline the kids. Jim wondered about his spiritual well-being and how to make his second marriage work, since he was once again encountering some of the same problems he had experienced in the first marriage, as well as some new ones — including an unhealthy dose of guilt and shame.

This chapter is primarily about the marriage relationship. However, you should seek to become an expert at relationships in general. This will open doors to you in life and business that nothing else will. Love is irresistible. The popularity of social media proves that. People love to connect with others — and talk about themselves. They are fascinated with themselves and enjoy being affirmed. No verbal statement you can make to anyone will be more powerful and compelling than letting them know by your actions that you care about them. Do you listen carefully when they speak to you? Do you remember and use their names? Do you truly seek to help them if they need it?

For the interest you show in people to yield meaningful results, it must be honest. Knowledge and mastery come naturally to some people in the area of relationships but may take others many years and diligent effort to develop. Good relationship skills are worth the time they take to develop. Relationships are crucial to opportunity, success, and happiness. If you find it easy to make friends, and if people want to be around you, then rejoice. If not, you need to learn some people skills. Everything important in life is a team effort.

After you discover your own weaknesses and blind spots, and you realize that you are not always right and certainly not perfect, and you are able to see another person's point of view, then you are in a starting position to consider a spouse. If you are considering marriage, then you should spend a long time courting — without sex — and a lot of time in prayer. Many believe that there is a "soul mate" for each and every person on earth. Others believe you can make a relationship work with almost anyone. I will not attempt to definitively answer that question here. Our God is a God of infinite detail. You should spend some time seeking someone He made especially for you, and if you are willing to work at it, then you will have marital happiness — eventually.

Do not fall into the trap of believing that if you struggle in marriage, you do not have the right partner. This is not the case. As two people become one, there will always be major adjustments, perhaps on a recurring basis. Fear not, because every marriage has issues that must be dealt with. Marriage and other important relationships will be full of adjustments and compromises. In marriage a key to success is to put your spouse first and seek their happiness above your own. Some couples will naturally be more compatible than others, but over time, couples grow closer as the natural ebb and flow of close contact and mutual experiences run their course.

There are some good indicators that you can assess when getting ready to choose your mate. Foremost, you should both have a similar faith and a willingness to put God first. Having a common purpose is the next most important thing in my mind. The best and highest purpose of a person or a couple is to serve God together. Make sure you are equally yoked in this respect. For many couples, the only common purpose will be the raising of children. This is fine, but obviously that purpose will wane as the children grow up and leave the home.

Even among Christians, there are different speeds and preferences between Christian partners for which adjustments must be made. For example, one may not want to go to church or may only want to attend once weekly, while the other enjoys attending church every time the doors are open. One partner may be reserved in their worship, while the other is demonstrative; one may be an introvert in Christian fellowship interactions, while the other may be an extrovert; one may love to give tithes and offerings freely and generously, while the other complains about it.

A typical young person who is a Christian may seek a marriage partner too hastily in order to engage in sexual activity without sinning. Here is a news flash for you: Marriage is not all about sex. Eventually the intense feelings of physical attraction fade. The realities of living 24/7 with another person — the same person for the rest of your life — will become very obvious with the passing of time. At that point, you can only hope you have chosen wisely. No one has a more powerful influence on you, your career, or your children, than your spouse does.

You should be established in your life's calling or career before marriage if possible. It is best to be financially secure — or at least on the path to financial security — because money issues are a major factor in marital stress. You cannot live on love. You should have similar ideas about the timing and the number of children you will have and how you will raise them, whether both partners will work or someone will stay home with the children, which church you will attend, compatibility with each other's families, significant political views, energy levels, recreational preferences, personal habits.

Do your due diligence, because you will bond with some people much more quickly and completely than you will with others based on these and other factors. Sometimes it's bonding, and sometimes it's simply tolerating. I prefer bonding based on mutually shared habits and preferences. But in any case, get ready, because you will no doubt still encounter troubles and difficulties that arise as the process of "becoming one" continues.

In Ecclesiastes 4:9, we read that "two are better than one." When one falls down, the other is there to help pull them back up. It is critical to find someone supportive, agreeable, and an advocate for you. Remember that a divided house cannot stand; but where two or more agree about anything they ask for, it will be done for them by God the Father. You are looking for a help mate — someone who will stand in your court and support you when no one else does. This person will be the one who brings out the best in you, and you will bring out the best in them. You should be pulling on the rope in the same direction.

Definitely hold off on sex until after marriage. Sex clouds the issue of compatibility assessment during courtship and replaces it with a sense of obligation to continue the relationship. Though it may be hard to believe, in my experience, physical attraction and sexual need are among the less important reasons when picking a spouse. In Ecclesiastes 1:9, Solomon said, "That which has been is what will be, that which is done is what will be done, and there is nothing new under the sun." Your intense attraction to one another is no different from the attraction felt by every other couple in the billions of other relationships that have occurred before yours; so follow God's laws regarding sex, and you will get the best results.

One of Satan's greatest tricks is to cause you to feel that you are different from everyone else and that your love is the most special love that has ever existed, entitling you to take special liberties before marriage and not to have to work hard at marriage. Satan will tell you that your pre-marital relationship is unique and unlike any other that has ever been on the face of the earth, so you are entitled to certain privileges. He will tell you that things that happen to other people will never happen to you. But keep your guard up and follow the time-honored principles found in Scripture.

You both should seek to understand the opposite sex and how to attend to their needs. Men mostly want unconditional love and sexual contact. Women primarily want unconditional love and communication.[24] Men tend to see themselves and judge themselves as providers, and often ignore the relationship aspects such as listening, security, or non-sexual touch. Women tend to be better at relationships. The bottom line in my mind is to marry someone you don't mind being around in a non-sexual

---

[24] 5. Top of The List. Five Love Needs Of Men And Women. Bible.org. https://bible.org/seriespage/5-top-list-five-love-needs-men-and-women.

environment 24/7. If you find that, then you are on the right track. I honestly think the ministries today emphasize sex too much, giving people the expectation that they are entitled to a great sex life in marriage or that they have a right to be "happy." Such is an honorable goal, no doubt; but it's not the main thing, and as you get older, it can become more challenging.

Pornography before or during marriage is a great mistake. It causes men to think that women are wired much differently than they actually are. Women can prefer many things more than sexual activity. It is difficult for a happily married Christian woman to compare herself to one of the "actors" in a pornographic situation because, in real life, all women are not wired that way. It is not the way God made them. Real life is very different. Additionally, sexual experiences before marriage can lead people to start comparing their experiences with different sexual partners. This is not helpful.

What is true biblical love? See 1 Corinthians 13 for God's definition of *agape* or unconditional love at the beginning of this chapter. Is love at first sight really possible? Probably not, at least not from the 1 Corinthians 13 point of view. True love is a daily decision, which makes it technically impossible to fall out of love. But, of course, it depends on your definition of love. Marital love takes years to develop and grow. Love is much sweeter after you have grown together and learned to pick your battles — and to avoid most of them. Lust, on the other hand, is easy to have at first sight and very hard to maintain over the years.

Beware of the marital role models you have seen on television or elsewhere in the world. As a man, how should you lead in the home? Many husbands abdicate their leadership role to their wives by default. Some men tend to live in the past and in the future, and rarely focus on the present. They can be perceived by their wives as uninterested, causing undue attention. Men tend to be distracted by their jobs and other stresses of life, not totally involved in the present moment with their wives or children. When this happens, women can feel unfulfilled in the home, and their emotional needs may be unmet. This may result in frequent arguments or nagging — or even seeking fulfillment in romance novels or other relationships. The husband may misperceive the source of his wife's behavior as disrespect that he does not deserve, reminding himself that he is a great provider and is working hard for the family. He may tell himself that other people would appreciate him more. He also may seek love and fulfillment elsewhere.

If your own personal happiness is your goal in marriage, then you probably will be disappointed. Do not marry in order to become happy or for personal fulfillment — only God can do that for you. So get that established first. Remember not to put too much pressure on your mate to meet your needs. Your mate is not required to meet all of your needs at all times, nor is this individual capable of doing so. Only God can meet all of your needs. If you seek fulfillment from God alone, and you seek to serve your mate and put their happiness above yours, you will not be disappointed, and your marriage will very likely succeed. Ultimately, a successful and enduring marriage, like so much else, is a daily decision.

A quick observation about arguing with your spouse, or anyone else, for that matter: It almost never has a good result. But if you do engage in a discussion, remember that your mind goes through ideas that are impacting the discussion much faster than you can speak them. To communicate effectively, it is important to take your time and convey everything associated with the issue if possible. Don't assume that you can speak ten words and adequately convey the history behind your feelings. Create the context of your position for best results and encourage your spouse to feel what you feel in the matter at hand. Remember that people think much faster and more fluently than they can communicate verbally.

In this chapter we do discuss finding the mate best suited for you. However, people grow together, and time and effort will make you very close if you both are willing to try. You should marry with the firm conviction that you will not divorce. If you know your own and your partner's tendencies as man and woman, and if you have developed your individual relationships with God, that is a great start. If you set realistic expectations, pick for compatibility as wisely as you can, and are willing to work hard under any circumstances, there should be no reason for divorce.

Kids should have both a mom and a dad in their lives, because each parent brings different perspectives and shows different sides of God — and reveals by example the various required life-skills. You must seek not to divorce. However, if divorce occurs, do not believe that God's forgiveness is denied to you. And do not believe Satan's lie that the kids are doomed to turn out badly. You must fight for and expect a good result when raising your children in a divorced situation in the exact same manner as you would if everything were absolutely perfect. Divorced people should encourage the kids to be involved with all parties and should never negatively influence the kids to side against one parent or the other. It's bad for the kids.

Do not buy into Satan's lie that things must be inferior or second rate in your lives or with your kids from that time forward. God is not against you. Once again, success in this area will lie in your decision not to let discouraging lies come in and affect your decisions when raising your children. Some examples might be parents tolerating bad behavior because the kids don't have both parents all the time, or parents being overly generous with gifts and privileges to make up for their perceived parental failures. This can result in behavioral dysfunction.

One other quick note about divorce: One of the most unpleasant feelings for a human is rejection. Divorce causes the feeling of rejection in both partners. Additionally, if remarriage and new families are involved, then there may be some sense of rejection on the part of the children and the new parent. This will have to be addressed. There is built-in pain that must be worked through pretty much everywhere you look. Divorce is not recommended. The Bible tells us that God hates it (see Malachi 2:16). Those who have experienced divorce know its many negatives.

The issues of divorce and remarriage are areas of much discussion in the church today. There are biblical grounds for divorce and remarriage that essentially justify these behaviors in the minds of *most* theologians; and there are other more trivial reasons, which usually qualify as sin. If you are struggling with issues of guilt, confusion, or shame after remarriage, seek pastoral guidance. Do what God tells you to do, because there are more opinions on this issue than almost any other. It's a very controversial topic, so try to avoid it.

The biblical mandate is clear. Marriage is very important to God. As Paul the Apostle says, go forward in the state you are in now, honoring your current marital status, and living for God as best you can (see Romans 7:27). Make no more mistakes in this area. Make whatever amends are possible and bear fruit in keeping with repentance. Remember that true repentance is in the heart — and is borne out by the firm resolve not to make the same mistakes again. *Stick to what the Bible says* on this subject.

As a parent, never show favoritism or make comparisons. This is especially true in blended families. Be careful to overcome debilitating sins and weaknesses before you pass them to your kids. Deal with your character flaws and other known weaknesses, and do not model them to your children. For successful relationships and a happy marriage, seek to avoid becoming offended. 1 Peter 4:8 says that love covers a multitude of sins. Nowhere is this truer than in marriage. When your spouse feels loved, you will find him or her being generally happier with everything you do. And when they do not feel loved, you can expect that they will be generally unhappier with everything you do.

Finally, the Bible talks of specific roles for husbands and wives. Wives should submit to their husbands, and husbands should love their wives as Christ loved the church and was willing to die for it (see Ephesians 5:25). The Bible also advises mutual submission for all Christians, not dominance (see 1 Peter 5:3). It is typical in my experience that husbands and wives who are submitting to one another almost always feel that they are doing what the other one wants, as opposed to what they individually want. This is the optimal situation. The man should love and cherish the woman, and the woman should honor and respect the man in return. This makes a great self-energizing cycle of happiness in a marital union.

I have experienced everything in this chapter and in fact learned most of it the hard way. I have also heard these concepts affirmed by many pastors and teachers and believe them to be reliable. There are several good marriage ministries that can teach you many useful steps to success. For those who would like further information on preparing for or improving their marriages, I recommend, among others, Jimmy and Karen Evans' *Marriage Today* materials.[25]

---

[25] Jimmy and Karen Evans. Marriage Today. https://marriagetoday.com/.

Chapter 14
Are Grace and Mercy That Big of a Deal?

John made much progress in his Christian walk. He loved the Lord and thought about Him all the time. He prayed daily and enjoyed Bible-related disciplines. He tried to be a good example to others of what a Christian should be, yet he continued to struggle with his thought life and the tendencies of the flesh. Every time he did not measure up to his own Christian standards — or felt guilty because of something he heard on the television or in church from a minister, reminding him of a past issue in his life — he became discouraged. He was especially discouraged when he had a thought or a desire to do something he had not done in years. "How could this still happen in my mind after all this time?" he wondered.

Since John was raised on the religious "do good, get blessed; do bad, get cursed" philosophy, he constantly worried if God still loved and accepted him whenever he failed. If something negative happened in his life near a time that he felt he had not lived up to God's commandments, he immediately concluded that it was God punishing him and that he had to "hit the reset button" by confessing and repenting to reestablish his relationship with God.

John would stop every so often during the day, close his eyes, and confess the sins of the last few minutes to God so he could restore his "broken fellowship." He wondered how he could ever be holy enough to enter heaven, even though he knew that was not how it worked. Almost every day he wondered what God thought about him, and if God still loved and accepted him when he made a mistake, said a "stray word," or committed a willful — or accidental — sin. John struggled with a performance-based theology, related to his acceptance by God, from early in his life, and he just could not break free.

> **Titus 2:11–14:** "For the grace of God that brings salvation has appeared to all men, teaching us that, denying ungodliness and worldly lusts, we should live soberly, righteously, and godly in the present age, looking for the blessed hope and glorious appearing of our great God and Savior Jesus Christ, who gave Himself for us, that He might redeem us from every lawless deed and purify for Himself His own special people, zealous for good works."
>
> **Hebrews 4:16:** "Let us therefore come boldly to the throne of grace, that we may obtain mercy and find grace to help in time of need."
>
> **Ephesians 2:4–5:** "But God, who is rich in mercy, because of His great love with which He loved us, even when we were dead in trespasses, made us alive together with Christ (by grace you have been saved)."

This chapter is about changing your perspective from one of performing works, in order to seek God's acceptance, to one of accepting His mercy and His grace-based love and approval, and serving Him through love and gratitude. This is a critical personal transition of immense importance.

When you start out in life, your perspective is one of self. Self-centeredness is the cause of many unpleasant emotions and actions. A constant focus on self will ruin your marriage, your relationships with other people, and your enjoyment of life and God. Selfishness is part of the baser side of human nature and can be made worse by fear of loss. Love, on the other hand, springs from faith that you are in good standing with the King of the universe. From my experience, I know that learning to be a great lover of God and others can be one of the hardest things in life; but it is the best way to be successful in serving God, your family, and your fellow man. Love is really the key to success in the Christian life. Love starts when we realize that God first loved us, as evidenced by the free gift of God — forgiveness of our sins by His mercy and salvation by grace through faith in the finished work of Jesus Christ.

If you can see things the way God sees them, you can learn what is really important to Him. God desires that the whole world should hear the gospel, believe on His Son, and be discipled into fruitful servants. The servant of Christ who is focused on self, and is constantly in some form of competition to do better *in order to gain or keep God's favor,* is missing the opportunity afforded by mercy and grace to truly rest and please God by faith working through love. They are not resting in what God has done for them and may be constantly striving for acceptance.

Just as success in business depends in part on knowing what is important to your boss and making it your priority, success as a Christian in the service of God depends on knowing and understanding what is truly important to God and pursuing it with all your heart. He wants you to rest in His provision of forgiveness and grace, and serve Him and others with gladness and gratitude. You must have His perspective. He wants you to enter the believer's rest — a rest based on trust and faith in a loving Father. That's where it all starts. That is the foundation of the building. Don't put the cart (your lifestyle as a Christian) before the horse (the completed work of Christ).

Let's look for a few moments at the wonderful phenomenon called "grace." Jesus Christ died so that we would, upon placing our faith in Him, be declared righteous in an instantaneous and unending transaction. Though humankind died to God because of Adam's sin in the garden, upon our asking Jesus to be our Savior, God the Father looks at us as His own sons and daughters *again.* We are in fact, "born again" unto Him. As He was pleased with Jesus, He is pleased with those of us who have entered into a faith relationship with Him by trusting in Jesus. He counts our debts as paid in full forever because of His mercy.

If your theology causes you to focus on yourself to ensure holiness at all times, then you will never really love and trust God, and you will never really desire to serve others from correct motives. You will more likely always be self-focused, trying to ensure that you are right with God — not a great witnessing trait. Most Christians have been raised and trained in typical religious traditions that put the requirements of righteousness and acceptance by God on the person rather than on God Himself through Christ. When such Christians are taught the grace message, they willingly receive it and happily acknowledge that they are now saved by grace as a gift from God. Yet they soon begin to assess their ongoing performance as if they could lose their standing with God through sin at any time. Thankfully, loss of salvation through sin is not possible for a true believer whose heart is sincerely toward God.

The message, as described by the apostle Paul in the book of Galatians is that we are saved initially by grace through faith, and we continue on by grace through faith alone. Paul says that if we could be saved by the works of the Law, then Christ came to earth and died in vain, clearly making the point that Christ had to come to accomplish what the Law could not accomplish. The Law simply sealed our sad fates, as no one is able to truly keep it. To new believers being influenced by the religious leaders of gospel times, who emphasized keeping the Law unto salvation, Paul asks: "Who has bewitched you? Having begun in the Spirit, are you now being made perfect by the flesh?" (Galatians 3:1, 3). This challenge is further developed in the book of Galatians.

While religion and the way of the world itself reinforce a conditional acceptance and a focus on self and performance, the message of grace supports our unconditional acceptance by God because of Christ. The message of grace is all about what Christ did for us, not about what we are doing for Him. It is unconditional and permanent acceptance by God for the true believer. Of course, this arouses the common objection, "Does that mean we can do whatever we want and still be saved?" Paul says, "God forbid" (see Romans 6:1).

Re-read Titus 2:11–14. If you have truly asked for and received salvation by faith and have received God's mercy, sinning is not your goal, nor is it enjoyable in the long run. We all know that sin is not a pleasurable event when you belong to God, because He chastises those who are His own. As many of us know, chastisement is a painful process. As you progress through the life of faith and the Spirit of God trains and develops you, as He inevitably does, your love for God grows and your desire for sin diminishes. The realization that you are truly heaven-bound inspires you to be the best you can be. Temptation will come, but the prospect of sinning loses much of its luster once you have accepted the fact that

God really loves you and will not forsake you. This is grace — the gift of God's acceptance.

Live your life focused on God and His Word, not on yourself and your performance. Accept His free gift of righteousness through faith, and His mercy in not giving you what you deserve. Let your joy manifest itself in loving obedience and service. You will not be judged for your sin if you are in Christ. Save your emotional energy for things that really matter instead of constantly re-assessing your established standing with God. Try to see yourself and the events of your life from God's perspective. With God, motive makes all the difference in reward. When Christ judges your works at the *Bema,* or Mercy Seat, good works motivated by love will be worth far more than anything "good" you do based upon your fear and your flesh. You can read more about the judgment of the believer at this location.[26]

Focus on really knowing that God loves you. Focus on putting your faith in Him as opposed to your own behavior or what you are doing for Him. Die to self and let Christ live through you. Rest in His mercy, which prevents your destruction, and the grace He has provided in Jesus Christ. Grace is among many other gifts we do not deserve, God's empowerment to fearlessly obey our Lord. We can forget our failures and move forward.

---

[26] The Doctrine of Rewards: The Judgment Seat (Bema) of Christ. Bible.org. https://bible.org/article/doctrine-rewards-judgment-seat-bema-christ.

Chapter 15
Some Tips for Succeeding in College or Trade School

As John's kids approached college, he offered them advice based on his years of experience and the wisdom he had learned from Scripture. He knew that most kids either lose their faith or have it greatly challenged in college, if not in high school. John knew that his kids needed to be prepared in advance before entering an environment where there are typically very few influences reinforcing the Christian faith.

John knew his kids would have to be deliberate, intentional, and active to maintain a strong faith in a liberal, primarily anti-religious environment where a great majority of students actually celebrate many behaviors that the Bible calls sinful. Biblical creation or intelligent design would be denounced in favor of evolution, which is supposedly scientifically supportable. John knew this would lead to his kids questioning the moral authority of all Scripture. They would wonder if the creation story was false and, if so, what other Bible teachings would be unreliable as guidance for their lives?

College is a good idea — if your discovered purpose requires that you obtain a college degree. However, if you decide to go to college, keep in mind that many tradesmen make a very good living without a college degree — and that many college graduates struggle to find work. Additionally, those who will take loans for college can amass a great debt burden and will need a good job after college to pay off their loans.

At college, expect your beliefs and morals to be challenged — even in a Christian college. You are responsible to make good choices right from the very beginning. You should immediately get yourself into a good church fellowship. There are also many Christian college student organizations that you can join. Get yourself into the habit of spending time in regular prayer and Bible reading each day, preferably in the morning, so that you do not get busy with other activities first. Whatever you plan to do first thing in the morning almost always gets done. Start each day with God, which is another form of first fruits, or giving the first portion of everything valuable to God. This discipline will keep you on track during your time at college. Many young people lose their faith in the secular university environment, if not during high school. You will have to be intentional about keeping your faith strong both before and during college.

Learning and preparation for your future is your *job* while you are in college. Work as hard while in college or trade school as you would expect to in your profession. College is not merely an opportunity to party and waste your parents' money. You are there to become persons of influence, with the ability to help others and share the gospel in the name of Christ through love.

That which you become very good at will be how you make your living. You will probably not become very successful and influential by being minimally good at many things — a "jack of all trades." You will more likely become successful and influential by being excellent at one thing. Many students graduate from college and are unable to find a job. Plan ahead, pick your study areas wisely, and become excellent at what you will one day do for a living. Choose your academic and career pursuits wisely, because your work in these pursuits may sustain you for the rest of your life.

If life at college wears you down physically or emotionally, which it occasionally will, you may become vulnerable to sinking into old, or new, sinful habits you believe will give you some comfort. Remember that destructive habits never helped you before, and while they may offer you some temporary distraction, they will only lead to bigger problems. If you find that you have made some mistakes, the correct course of action is to immediately begin to do the next right thing. Do what you know is right, even if you don't feel like it. Then keep at it — until you *do* feel like it.

Sin never helped anybody, so consistently do the right things. When you get discouraged, don't focus on your sin or failures, lest your sadness, guilt, and shame lead you to worse behavior. Do not focus downward or inward. Rather, focus upward to God. When you focus on God and His grace, you will be encouraged in your Christian walk. When you focus on your behaviors, your sin, your do's and don'ts, you are more likely to fail again. Learn to fall in love with God and die to self.

Your habits create your destiny. Do the things each and every day that will cause you to achieve your goals. The trend or habit is more important than any individual activity. If you study each day, if you sleep well each night, if you eat well each day, or if you exercise each day, you'll find that these good behaviors will eventually bring you to your desired place. Such behaviors also tend to improve your mental attitude.

Make sure to get connected. **Go to all of your classes and get involved with others through activities.**

The Bible tells us that when we are saved, the Lord gives us the Comforter to go with us (see John 14:16). The Comforter, as you know, is the Holy Spirit of God. He dwells within you if you are a Christian. He will not leave you or forsake you, and He will be a comforter and a friend, if you let Him. Be still, unclutter your mind, and listen to the still small voice of God. Just go forward one step at a time. Most of the things you are worried about will never happen. Remember that your thoughts impact your choices and create your future. The good news is that you can change your thought patterns. Don't let negative thoughts influence your decisions.

In the first thirty days of school, just as in the first thirty days of anything, establish good habits via routine, and they will tend to persist. Set up good routines for worship, study, and social life. Get into a good fellowship and set up some daily disciplines that you will follow. First thing in the morning, have a short devotional, consisting of prayer, Bible reading, thanksgiving, and praise. Don't try to make too many changes at once. Start small and get some quick wins. Set up a simple routine and a few simple rules to follow. Remember, God is your Father. He loves you and is not keeping score, hoping you fail. You are doing these things for your own good, not to impress God.

Choose a good roommate if you can, because he or she will be a strong influence on your life. In terms of getting along with roommates, it's helpful to remember that guys tend to run away when conflict arises, whereas girls tend to work through it. Unless the issues are legal, moral, or ethical, plan to work through them. After the beginning of any relationship, as things progress, there is always a time of struggle. Try not to get offended.

Expect to have constructive confrontations in life, even welcome them, but don't let them get too personal. Fight fair. Pride and selfishness ruin friendships and marriages, so avoid them both. Paul advises us: "In lowliness of mind let each esteem others better than himself. Let each of you look out not only for his own interests, but also for the interests of others" (Philippians 2:3–4). In your house or room, if you see that something needs to be done, just do it. Do not expect the other person to read your facial expressions and "get the message."

The world of the next twenty to thirty years will be characterized by an aging United States and world population that will no doubt need more medical and pharmaceutical care.[27] As the economy becomes more globally interconnected, the medical, scientific, and engineering professions, as well as business and financial services, may be in high demand for people here in the US. Do an Internet search to see which professions are projected to be most relevant in the future. If one of these professions matches your skills and interests, then it would be a good one to pursue. Again, it is important to be intentional. Don't wait for answers to drop out of the sky. Carefully choose the right academic areas to focus on.

It could be wise to learn a second language. Many people around the world will enter the middle class in the next ten years, and that may drive many US and multinational companies to greater prosperity. Be prepared to be a vital part of that. You must be strong and successful in order to help others who need the gospel and physical aid, and to provide well for your family.

Seek wisdom in making your life choices. Choose your path well. Study a specific area in depth and become excellent at it. Your purpose is to serve God with gladness and accomplish His purposes, powered by love. Your enemy is Satan. Abiding in Christ occurs in many choices a day. But fear not, because your enemy is defeated by the blood of the

---

[27] Wikipedia Contributors. Demographic profile. https://en.wikipedia.org/wiki/Demographic_profile.

Lamb, Jesus Christ. You need only to walk in that victory, armed with the knowledge of the tricks of the evil one and knowing that you will always have a way of escape. Look up, not inward, for your God and His grace are the victory.

In preparing for your career, work on your strengths. Don't worry too much about your weaknesses — except perhaps those weaknesses that directly support your strengths, like speaking or reading better — because you will eventually be part of a team. You can look to your passions, or you can look to your gifts. If possible, look to both. If you must pick one of these to base your career on, you would probably be better off to pick a career based on your natural gifts, talents, and interests so you will perform best. Learn all you can and be diligent. If you are good at what you do and you work hard, the Bible says that you will stand before kings (Proverbs 22:29). In your career, if possible, **surround yourself with a team of people who excel in those things you do not do well. Teams achieve the greatest accomplishments.**

What about failure? Do not be afraid to fail, because it may prevent you from trying at all. Failure is not only unavoidable, but it's also a major part of the path to success. It is actually a good thing, because it teaches you. Don't be afraid to tackle new and difficult things. Soon you will master them if you do not quit. Spending a few minutes a day, every day, you can learn or accomplish almost anything. Most people do not realize this, and they think they must master something all at once. Life does not work that way. If you are interested, research to see how many greatly successful people failed often, and badly, before achieving success — people like Abraham Lincoln.

There may be weaknesses in your life that can derail you — depression, addiction, lust, guilt, worry, fear. When temptation hits, submit yourself to the Lord and resist the devil by speaking Scripture against the temptation; then get busy with something or someone and tell yourself you can make it. Go out and be around other people. Call an accountability partner or help somebody else with a problem. Plan your success ahead of time. You should expect that Satan will use certain things to trigger the thoughts and emotions that lead to sin. Learn to avoid them or deal with them.

Being alone extensively is a sure way to get tempted or depressed.

So is going to the wrong places with the wrong people. Get connected with the right people, and stay connected. Don't expect temptation to completely leave you, but do expect victory in the promise that "God is faithful, who will not allow you to be tempted beyond what you are able, but with the temptation will also make the way of escape, that you may be able to bear it" (1 Corinthians 10:13).

Learn to "just say no," and you will save yourself a lot of trouble. Adam lost, Samson lost, and even David lost by saying "yes" to the devil's tricks. Of course, thank God, they all ultimately won in the end, but I am sure that they would have preferred to get a do-over. Just say "no" and go do something else. God will provide a way of escape if you are willing to take it. You cannot beat the devil by yourself. You have a warrior on your side: Jesus Christ. Rely on His strength to succeed and on His mercy and second chances when you fail.

Remember this key to success in life: The best way to get consistently good behavioral results is to plan to avoid the wrong situations. Control your choices and your surroundings and decide to win in advance. Don't go to places where sinful activities occur. Don't watch sinful or provocative things in movies or on television, thinking you won't succumb to their influences. Don't associate with friends who routinely make bad choices. Do not extensively associate with anyone whom you do not want to be like in some way. Your close associates will influence you, whoever they are. 1 Corinthians 15:33 says: "Do not be deceived: 'Evil company corrupts good habits.'" This scripture appears to indicate that it is far more likely that a person determined to do wrong will negatively influence someone trying to do right, than the other way around.

Choose optimal places to study. Sometimes your room is not the best place to study, especially if friends or roommates are present. Go somewhere quiet for better concentration. Use the library, the study hall in the dorm, or a class area to study. Then go to your room when you are ready to relax. And if you need help be sure to get it from professors, qualified friends, or tutors.

When you go to class, do not follow the herd. Many will go to the back of the lecture hall to gain anonymity — or to be cool. Sit near the front. Raise your hand. Ask and answer questions. Visit each professor at least once and address him or her with respect: "Professor," "Sir."

"Ma'am." The more motivated students are probably sitting in front. Get into study groups with people who want to do well and make friends with them.

Here are three good steps for preparing for class: 1) Before class, read what's coming in the next lesson; 2) go to class and take decent notes — or purchase or borrow them; and 3) read the notes you took in class again that night. That completes one cycle. Repetition is key to retaining information. Review the information in your mind. Write it. Speak it. Teach it to yourself. These are all more effective forms of learning than just listening casually once in class. Think of learning as a lifelong experience and consider it a privilege that you enjoy while at college, courtesy of Mom and Dad — or your Uncle Sam! This will be even more obvious to you if you are one of the few paying for your own education.

In your spiritual life, you can teach yourself that you want and need to follow God, but you may still be drawn in the wrong direction by your passions and emotions until you train them. You can influence your emotions by looking at the experience of Bible characters or real-life persons who followed God all their lives and comparing their life experiences with those who chose their own way and met with difficulties. Discipline yourself with a few good habits and rules to guide your life in the right direction. People can read the Bible or Christian books full of advice and never change. You have to apply the advice.

Keep it simple. Decide on some steps to follow — like the ones mentioned in this chapter. Do any of them, or all of them. Start your habits in the first thirty days. Find a good church fellowship as soon as possible. Find a good Christian student organization to join. Daily prayer and Bible-reading disciplines early in the morning are essential, no matter how short. You can watch Christian TV in the morning or before bed. Many Christian networks have great shows in the morning and in prime time. Listen to Christian radio. Perhaps let it play all the time in your room, as a roommate of mine once did. Use music to start your prayer time in the morning if you need to. Talk about God with others and wisely choose your environment and personal associations. You have to be deliberate.

Finally, and perhaps most importantly, you should be confident that the Bible is the way to go. You should be confident from Scripture and other sources that the creation story is valid and that evolution — the soup to man version — is not supportable. You should become confident that Bible stories are true and, in many cases, have been proven through discovery. Resources such as Josh McDowell's *Evidence that Demands a Verdict* and Ken Ham's *Answers* series, the writings of creation evangelist Kent Hovind, and many others can help you resolve these concerns and give you confidence that you are on the right path if you believe and follow God's word as written. There is nothing more faith-shaking than being challenged by some of the skeptics at college — and then finding that you lack the necessary grounding in Scripture from which to counter their challenges.

> **Ecclesiastes 12:13–14:** "Let us hear the conclusion of the whole matter: Fear God and keep His commandments, for this is man's all. For God will bring every work into judgment, including every secret thing, whether good or evil."

Here, once again, is wisdom from the richest man who ever lived: King Solomon, a great king of Israel. He had more money and possessions than anyone in the world. And when he concluded the book of Ecclesiastes, these were his words. A wise man learns from other people's mistakes. Read Solomon's words and take them to heart. Stand on the shoulders of Solomon, David, Samson, and so many others who have learned that God's way is indeed the best way. Learn to take God at His word early in life.

Chapter 16
Are Miracles and Healings Still Happening Today?

1 Corinthians 12:7–11: "But the manifestation of the Spirit is given to each one for the profit of all: for to one is given the word of wisdom through the Spirit, to another the word of knowledge through the same Spirit, to another faith by the same Spirit, to another gifts of healings by the same Spirit, to another the working of miracles, to another prophecy, to another discerning of spirits, to another different kinds of tongues, to another the interpretation of tongues. But one and the same Spirit works all these things, distributing to each one individually as He wills."

Mark 16:17–18: "And these signs will follow those who believe: In My name they will cast out demons; they will speak with new tongues; … they will lay hands on the sick, and they will recover."

Isaiah 53:5: "But He was wounded for our transgressions, He was bruised for our iniquities; the chastisement for our peace was upon Him, and by His stripes we are healed."

1 Peter 2:24: "Who Himself bore our sins in His own body on the tree, that we, having died to sins, might live for righteousness — by whose stripes you were healed."

It is always best to stay "prayed up" before an issue occurs. When living life, take appropriate precautions and be prudent. If you are sick, go to the doctor if you need to. It is wise to employ good eating and exercise habits to avoid getting sick in the first place, and to consistently pray for all of God's blessings, liberally applying all of the promises of God in His Word. Verbally declare God's good promises over your life. Always exercise your authority as a believer and seek to create the life you want by actively calling upon God's promises.

A miracle is something highly unusual or dramatic that cannot be explained by natural events. Examples of miracles might be a regenerated missing limb or someone raised from the dead. Far more often we see healings that should not necessarily be categorized as miracles according to the verses cited above. God provided for healing at the cross, just as He did for salvation. See Isaiah 53:5, for example, which declares that "by His stripes we are healed." This means physical healing, among other benefits. The Blue Letter Bible is a great resource that enables you to look up a word in the original language[28]. In doing so here we can see that the word *heal* means, among other things, to physically heal.

The Apostle John tells us that Jesus Christ was made manifest in order to destroy the works of the devil. In 1 John 3:8 we read, "He who sins is of the devil, for the devil has sinned from the beginning. For this purpose, the Son of God was manifested, that He might destroy the works of the devil." We might ask what the works of the devil are. According to Scripture, the works of the devil are sickness, sin, oppression, poverty, fear, lack, and every evil thing going on in the world.

The really good news is that Christ accomplished His mission and has won the victory over all of these things. Matthew 8:16–17 says, "And He cast out the spirits with a word, and healed all who were sick, that it might be fulfilled which was spoken by Isaiah the prophet, saying: 'He Himself took our infirmities and bore our sicknesses.'"

In John 17:4 Jesus says, "I have glorified You [God] on the earth. I have finished the work which You have given me to do." What prevents us from living in the full enjoyment of His accomplishment? There may be many things — some within our control, some not.

---

[28] Blue Letter Bible. https://www.blueletterbible.org/.

Those who have had bad things happen beyond their control should never blame themselves. God says in His Word that in this life there will be trouble, but we should not fear, for Christ has overcome the world (see John 16:33). God is ultimately in control, and we can call upon what He did for us to gain victory. In Romans 8:28, Paul says, "And we know that all things work together for good to those who love God, to those who are the called according to His purpose."

The successful formula for more frequently seeing healings and other victories over Satan is in biblical and Holy Spirit-given knowledge, faith, and the application of the Word and promises of God. God tells us in Hosea 4:6, "My people are destroyed for lack of knowledge." Again, we must never blame ourselves spiritually when bad things happen, but we can increase our chances of great victory if we understand what Christ did and we walk in faith accordingly, staying prayed up, expecting His word to be fulfilled. Just as we must have faith for salvation, we must have faith for healing and deliverance from all manner of evil. Our weapon is the Word of God — the Sword of the Spirit — and we wield it primarily with our mouths. Jesus provided complete victory for us at the cross.

When something bad — or even something terrible — does occur, it is a common theme among gospel ministers these days to say that God is not really in control. This seems to be a commonplace way of explaining how all the tragedies of life can occur. They explain that it is not God, but Satan who is the author of all evil. And, of course, that is absolutely true. Satan is, indeed, the responsible one. But they take it a step further by saying that God is simply not in control at all.

Some say, for example, that if God were in absolute control — controlling every action and occurrence — a criminal could not possibly be held responsible for his or her actions, and we should not put him or her in prison. While it is true that God does not control the individual actions of every man or woman on the face of the earth, minute by minute, it is also true that God is ultimately sovereign and in control and will work all things to the good for those who are the called according to His purpose and those who love Him.

When you read the book of Revelation, you can see that the outcome prophesied is the victory of our Lord Jesus Christ. We cannot be sure that this will occur if God is not in control. If God is not sovereign, then we have no guarantee where we will end up after our lives here on earth are over. Either God is ultimately in control, or He is not. Rest assured, though, that He is, and you can call on Him to perform His Word to help you prevail, or to help you endure.

When something bad happens in life, remember that God is in control — though He very likely did not cause that event or punish us with it, since the sacrifice of Jesus occurred, satisfying the penalty for sins. We must never question God's motives. Since God and free will have existed from the very beginning, it is obvious that evil existed from the very beginning.

Let me explain: If God is good, then not choosing Him is evil. Evil — the potential to disobey God — has existed as long as God has existed. So don't blame God for evil. Evil is the opposite of what God is and what God requires. Evil happens when people do not choose God. To our knowledge, evil was embodied in our realm when Satan rebelled against God and enticed humankind to sin. Satan began his work with the cooperation of humankind when Adam and Eve sinned against God in Eden.

Despite this sinful, broken world, God is responsible to work all things together for good — and He will do so. Whatever it is you face, He will help you through it. Even in the event of an untimely or emotionally painful death of a loved one, remember that it is hardest on those who are left behind. The Christian who has passed on is absolutely in a better place now and is free from pain and sorrow — as well as from the troubles of this world. So, in a sense, we are really grieving for ourselves, because we are the ones who remain here — without our loved ones.

> **Isaiah 57:1–2:** "The righteous perishes, and no man takes it to heart; Merciful men are taken away, while no one considers that the righteous is taken away from evil. He shall enter into peace; they shall rest in their beds, each one walking in his uprightness."

The Apostle Paul tells us not to grieve like the rest of humankind, who have no hope, but to comfort each other with these words: "But I do not want you to be ignorant, brethren, concerning those who have fallen asleep, lest you sorrow as others who have no hope. For if we believe that Jesus died and rose again, even so God will bring with Him those who sleep in Jesus" (1 Thessalonians 4:13–14).

> **2 Corinthians 5:8:** "We are confident, yes, well pleased rather to be absent from the body and to be present with the Lord."

When you are confronted with a very difficult situation, pray to see the situation from God's perspective and focus on the love and faithfulness of God. When a loved one is very sick, pray for healing with faith, and with the knowledge that God supports physical healing in all cases, and that He is not only able but also willing to heal. You are basically agreeing with God's Scriptures. The blood of our Savior Jesus Christ is more powerful than any disease or sickness. *Plead the blood of Jesus out loud* over any sickness and expect results. The blood cannot fail. I challenge you to try it.

When Christ was on earth, He and the apostles went about healing all who were afflicted with sickness and disease. The Scripture says that Jesus "bore our sins in His own body on the tree, that we, having died to sins, might live for righteousness — by whose stripes you were healed" (1 Peter 2:24). This healing is not only spiritual but also physical. The Greek word for salvation used in Scripture is sozo, which implies salvation, healing, and provision.[29] This is what God wants for us. Accordingly, we should pray that way in agreement. If healing does not come, then we must not blame ourselves or criticize our lack of faith and poor performance — as some preachers say — but, rather, keep on trusting and praying every time.

As Jesus told Jairus after people told him his daughter had died, "Do not be afraid; only believe" (Mark 5:36). When someone prays for healing and then feels sick again, they should not assume that the prayer has not been answered, but should continue to speak and act in faith, expecting to be healed over time in accordance with God's Word. When seeking God, remain in an attitude of expectancy and faith.

---

[29] Save - Sozo (Greek Word Study) | Precept Austin. www.preceptaustin.org/save_sozo_greek_word_study.

Today, as Christians, we have the Holy Spirit living in us, and we have a direct line to God when we pray. Daniel 9 and 10 show us some of the behind-the-scenes activity when we pray. From these scriptures, it is clear that demonic activity can affect our prayers — especially when those prayers relate to other people and things beyond our control. The message here is to keep praying and speaking in faith without wavering. Also, specifically pray against any opposition, hindrance, or evil influence impacting your prayers. Good things can take time. Use your authority in Christ to speak against the spirits that may hinder your answers and the results you desire.

Trust in God and in His love. See the event from His viewpoint. Remember that to live is Christ and, if it happens, to die is gain (see Philippians 1:21). God Himself suffered the loss of His only begotten Son, Jesus, on our behalf. Pray the Scriptures relevant to your situation and remember God's past faithfulness to His children. Fill your mind with the realization of God's love for you. Visualize your renewed health and well-being. Be willing to take authority over the issue you are praying about in Jesus' name.

When ministering to a sick person, you can employ James 5:14 and call upon your church elders to pray for this person and anoint them with oil in the name of the Lord. It likely will be best if those elders believe in healing. Call on Christ's sacrifice at the cross. Remind the sick person that we are promised long life and happiness. For younger folks, remind them that they are promised seventy or eighty years at least, according to the Bible (see Psalm 90:10). Ask them if they honor their father and mother, and if they do, remind them that they are promised by the Fifth Commandment a long life. Quote Psalm 91:10, which says, "Neither shall any plague come nigh thy dwelling." Take them through the Gospels, showing how Christ and the Apostles healed all who came to them. I have heard that Oral Roberts once said that to build up your faith for healing, you should pray as though everyone you have ever prayed for previously had been successfully healed.

There are many ministries that teach or emphasize healing. If you are struggling with illness and faith for healing, I would in particular recommend Andrew Wommack Ministries. It is a wonderful faith-building ministry and an excellent source of healing-related teaching

Biblical Principles for Successful Living

and inspiration. Andrew points out that lack of knowledge can prevent healing. The laws of God allow for healing, but some believers may not know enough to draw upon those laws. The healing testimonies and healing teachings on his website are very encouraging.[30]

A famous story about Charles Greenaway after he had lost his eight-year-old son ends with him saying, "I will not go to hell over a mystery."[31] So, the reason I am writing these things to you is to tell you this: do not assess everything from your own perspective. Rather, as Christians, assess things from the perspective of a loving God who deals in eternal matters. Use all the right principles in advance, and in the moment. Count on the faithful promises of God. Never work against yourself, and be persistent.

It is difficult to over-emphasize the importance of proper thinking that is in line with the Word of God, followed by consistently-expressed proper words from Scripture which exhort a certain outcome. Know what to expect from God, be determined to realize it in your situation, and leave all the results to Him. He really does want the best for us.

The bottom line is that healings and miracles are happening all over this world today. There are thousands of testimonies of documented miracles and healings. We ourselves are miracles. Our bodies, this world, and the universe are all essentially miracles seamlessly working every day. Did you know you are moving several thousand miles per hour right now? Every process in your body is a miracle of sorts. Believe and pray for miracles.

Prayer and faith are key, so build your faith to the point of explosion. Spend time building your faith by exposing yourself to believing mentors and, most importantly, to the Word of God. Watch testimonies of successful miracles, because we overcome by the Blood of the Lamb and the word of our testimony (see Revelation 12:11).

If you need a healing or a miracle but do not get it, do not blame yourself, as some Christians would tell you. Just keep going and try again the next time to pray and realize a healing or a miracle. Try, try, and try

---

[30] Andrew Wommack Ministries. https://www.awmi.net/series/healing/.
[31] Joe Tannous. Don't Go To Hell Over A Mystery. https://joetannous.wordpress.com/2015/12/10/dont-go-to-hell-over-a-mystery/.

again — until you get it a few times. Then watch your faith explode. Remember to always "plead the blood" of Jesus. Leave it in God's hands after claiming His promises as persistently and as faithfully as you can. Never quit — and never work against yourself with a negative confession. The Word will always be the Word, and it will not change.

When something comes to mind, pray about it. It may be that the Holy Spirit is leading you to pray what is on God's heart for someone else's healing. Learn to listen to what God brings to your mind and pray it back to God when ministering to people. When ministering to a sick person, explain the gospel to ensure that he or she knows the Lord. Show examples of healing in the Scriptures and from current testimonies, and see if their faith is growing. Ask God to tell you what to expect or to pray for in any particular case. Then pray for the person and leave the results to God. Healing may be immediate, or it may take time. The person should not be discouraged if symptoms return. Just keep expecting the eventual healing. God is the healer who said that we, as disciples, can do the things He did.

Spend as much time as you can with God each day. Play Christian music to get into a spirit of worship. Pray in tongues often, if that is something the Holy Spirit has given you. Be thankful and praise Him. Think of yourself as a capacitor storing up faith like electricity. Build your faith at all times by hearing and meditating in the Word. Don't let the world dissipate your faith. When the time for healing comes, remember that the Scripture says it is "the children's bread."[32] We are entitled to it. When the time for a miracle comes, remember that God loves you. Pray to Him through Christ with authority. Agree with His promises for healing and miracles. Leave all the results to Him, and never blame yourself if things do not go the way you want them to. Take the long view and just keep going. All things are possible with God. Never restrict His possibilities.

2 Timothy 3:5: "Having a form of godliness but denying its power. And from such people turn away!"

---

[32] Isaiah 53:5; Matthew 15: 21-28; Matthew 8:16-17 and 15:22-29; 1 Peter 2:24.

Chapter 17

What's Coming Next for This World and Us?

John wondered with great interest about prophecy. "Are we living in the last days? Will there be a rapture, or will Christians go through the tribulation period? How much time is left, and how should I prepare?"

People without a word from the Lord will be led easily into fear and despair. We need a word from God to know what will become of us. We need a word from the Lord to encourage us and give us assurance when times are hard or when the world seems most troubled. How do we get this word? The Bible tells us that just as our Savior Jesus was and is, we are prophets, priests, and kings, all in one. We can know things and prophesy into our own futures by staying in close contact with God and speaking His Word for us from the Bible as well as the *rhema* word we receive through prayer for our situations. God's Word is always prophetic and must always come to pass.

God wants to bless us, so we must agree with Him and speak those blessings and prophetic utterances from the Word of God for ourselves and our families frequently. This is a form of prophecy that anyone can apply. What is God saying to you in your prayer time? Make sure to listen. What does God say to you in Scripture about your issues and concerns? Should you fear anything? Should you worry? Are you the righteousness of God in Christ? Does the blood of Christ continually cleanse you? Remember that you have been redeemed from the curse of the Law and grafted in to the blessings of Abraham.

All of the blessings of Abraham and the children of Israel are ours in Christ, since we are grafted in. "Christ has redeemed us from the curse of the law, having become a curse for us (for it is written, 'cursed is everyone who hangs on a tree'), that the blessing of Abraham might come upon the Gentiles in Christ Jesus, that we might receive the promise of the Spirit through faith" (Galatians 3:13–14).

And in Genesis 12:2–3 we see God's promise to Abraham: "I will make you a great nation; I will bless you and make your name great; and you shall be a blessing. I will bless those who bless you, and I will curse him who curses you; and in you all the families of the earth shall be blessed."

What are some more of the blessings we can expect as believers? See Deuteronomy 28:1–14 for a long list of what God desires for us. Speak these blessings and all the promises of God always into your life, the lives of your children, and all of your situations. You are effectively prophesying.

There are hundreds of promises to God's people in Scripture. In many cases, these are for us today as well. The promises of God have been fulfilled and ratified in Christ. "For all the promises of God in Him are Yes, and in Him Amen, to the glory of God through us" (2 Corinthians 1:20).

Jesus Christ is our "Yes" and "Amen" for receiving the promises. Agree with Him and pray His Word back to Him. Meditate on the Scriptures for all that you need to accomplish His purposes. You are a speaking spirit, so confess and repent of previously-spoken negatives and help bring His will for your existence into your life. This is an exciting and wonderful life because we belong to Jesus Christ and the Word of God is our Prophet.

Discern your general and specific future purpose and declare it to be so verbally.

The Bible has a lot to say about what comes next after our lives here are over. One day we will rule and reign with Christ. 1 Corinthians 6:3 reads: "Do you not know that we shall judge angels? How much more, things that pertain to this life?" Revelation 2:26 reads, "And he who overcomes, and keeps my works until the end, to him I will give power over the nations."

> **1 Thessalonians 4:13-19:** "For the Lord Himself will descend from heaven with a shout, with the voice of an archangel, and with the trumpet of God. And the dead in Christ will rise first. Then we who are alive and remain shall be caught up together with them in the clouds to meet the Lord in the air. And thus we shall always be with the Lord."

The Bible speaks of a coming time of tribulation. Most Christian theologians believe it will last for seven years, with an especially terrible period in the second three and a half years.[33] Some believe it will be only three and a half years long, and still others say it will be an indeterminate time. These opinions are based on different readings of Daniel Chapter 9 and the seventy sevens of years in Daniel's vision.[34] Scripture is clear, however, that there will be a time of tribulation, and it will be a terrible time to be on earth — consisting of wars, famines, and natural disasters.

Will Christians endure this time, or will they be raptured? As far as the rapture, or calling out, is concerned, theologians are divided in their opinions. Some believe Christians will endure the tribulation period foretold in Revelation before being taken out. This is a post-tribulation rapture scenario and is principally supported, in my mind anyway, by Matthew 24 and 2 Thessalonians 2. It is also supported by the fact that in the case of the Mosaic deliverance from Egypt (the plagues) and the

---

[33] What is the Tribulation? Got Questions?
https://www.gotquestions.org/tribulation.html.
[34] What are the seventy weeks of Daniel?
https://www.gotquestions.org/seventy-weeks.html.

Noahic Flood, God's people were on the earth but were protected from calamity. This envisions a rapture or calling out of believers at the end of the tribulation period, followed closely by the return of Christ, with those who were raptured, to participate in a great battle called Armageddon.

Many others believe that Christians will not be here during the tribulation at all, because we will be taken out before it starts. This would be a pre-tribulation rapture. The pre-tribulation rapture is supported by verses which say believers will *avoid the wrath to come* — and the fact that Christ's second coming, which occurs at the end of the tribulation, and the rapture are treated in Scripture as two different events. They do not need to occur at the same time.

Both schools of thought agree that believers will avoid the wrath of God poured out near the end of the tribulation. But the tribulation period will have much trouble in it aside from the wrath of God. If we do not go through the tribulation, then we will be raptured and be with the Lord while unrivaled evil breaks loose on earth. If we do go through it, consider it an opportunity to share your faith with others at that time and be ready to be martyred for Christ. Be ready in either case. It should be noted that some theologians do not believe in a rapture at all, but feel that Christians will always remain here on earth through the second coming of the Lord.

In my opinion, Scripture clearly teaches that believers will avoid God's wrath to come, but terrifying times will come on earth before the Lord establishes His millennial kingdom on earth for a thousand years. Whether Christians will be here for any of these events is a matter only God knows at this point. It is wise for us all to make some mental and physical — not to mention spiritual — preparations, and to be ready.

After death, all people will experience one of two judgments. They will either experience the judgment of the believers at the *Bema,* or Mercy Seat, where they will be assured a place in heaven and be rewarded for deeds done on earth (see 2 Corinthians 5); or they will experience the Great White Throne judgment of unbelievers (see Revelation 20). There are differing opinions on this issue as well.[35] We do know for sure that believers will receive God's mercy.

---

[35] What is the Great White Throne Judgment? Got Questions. https://www.gotquestions.org/great-white-throne-judgment.html.

Then there is the issue of heaven and hell. The Bible clearly states that the followers of Christ receive eternal life and go to be with the Lord forever. Paul said that to be absent from the body is to be present with the Lord (see 2 Corinthians 5:8). Most believe this occurs immediately upon death. Others believe that Christians stay in the grave, "sleeping" until the first resurrection and the judgment of the believers.

Those who choose not to believe will absolutely experience eternal separation from God in a place called hell. Again, most believe that the experience of hell is one of eternal, unending fiery torment, while others believe that it is a one-time final death/destruction in fire for most people. In any event, the choice could not be clearer. Believers get to inherit eternal life and enjoy the Lord forever in the New Heaven and New Earth depicted in Revelation 21.

> **Romans 2:6–8:** "Who will render to each one according to his deeds: eternal life to those who by patient continuance in doing good seek for glory, honor, and immortality; but to those who are self-seeking and do not obey the truth, but obey unrighteousness — indignation and wrath."

There are many resources that unpack what to expect in the end times. Jane Holley recommends *The Last Things: An Eschatology for Layman* by George Ladd; *The Promise of the Future* by Cornelis Venema; and *The Return of Christ* by G. C. Berkouwer. Find and study a good theologically and biblically sound resource on the book of Revelation and end times prophecies. Revelation 1:3 promises a special blessing for the student of this book: "Blessed is he who reads and those who hear the words of this prophecy and keep those things which are written in it; for the time is near."

So, in sum, we have already seen the coming of Jesus as Messiah to His people Israel and His gift of eternal life also offered to Gentile believers who have been grafted in to God's chosen people; we have seen the rebirth of Israel as a nation in 1948, as foretold in the prophets; we have seen the City of Jerusalem returned to Jewish control in 1967; and we have seen it affirmed as Israel's capital in 2018 by the President of the United States. All we await is the rapture, the tribulation period, and the second coming of Jesus Christ and His thousand-year reign immediately after the Tribulation.

Again, there are various interpretations of end time events and the reader should really do their own research on this. According to the book of Revelation, the tribulation period will be a time of great suffering and disaster. It will end with the return of Christ and the establishment of the thousand-year reign of Jesus as King on earth, during which Satan is restricted to the bottomless pit (see Revelation 9). The thousand-year reign will be followed by the release of Satan, a final battle, and a final judgment. Then the New Heaven and the New Earth will be established, and we will be with the Lord forever. The message to us is that this occurrence is closer than ever — and we should be ready, with a strong faith in Jesus, living a life that reflects our faith. We must be ready to die for our faith if necessary — and ready to rule and reign with our Lord when He returns.

Seeing the upheaval that will be coming to earth and the eventual eternal disposition of all people, shouldn't we be especially diligent to share the wonderful good news of Christ with others while we still can? Be sure to do your part.

Chapter 18

Develop Amnesia When Necessary!

Some people have an excellent ability to forget the past and focus forward. This is no small gift. I have seen the great quarterbacks complete amazing plays shortly after terrible mistakes. They seem to know how to clear their heads, while others seem able to only focus on their past failures, crippling their concentration. Perhaps it is their past proven athletic abilities that give them the confidence to focus forward. For the Christian it should be our Savior's great mercies, which are new every morning, that encourage us.

The ability to not let the past drag down your future is essential to a happy and successful Christian life. Our brains love to dig up the past. It may be a learned behavior or a natural tendency, but many attribute this constant inclination to dwell on the negative to the influence of Satan and his demons, who continually place thoughts of condemnation, fear, doubt, worry, and sadness into our minds, causing distraction, negative expectations, and crippling destructive self-talk. People worry about everything imaginable.

Worry is meditating on fear-based thoughts, and it is the exact opposite of what we are supposed to be meditating on in faith — the Word of God. If you can do something about a troublesome situation, you should do so. If there is nothing you can do and you simply keep worrying, rather than giving it to God, you will be most miserable. The more you think about a negative outcome, the more your worry grows. The Bible's instruction is not to worry about anything but to pray about everything. Paul tells us in Philippians 4:6: "Be anxious for nothing, but in everything by prayer and supplication, with thanksgiving, let your requests be made known to God."

People can be especially subject to mental attack after a tragedy or a major negative experience such as sickness, job loss, or the death of a loved one. They can begin to feel vulnerable and doubt God's faithfulness.

Another entry point to our minds is the guilt and shame that hamper us after we commit a sin or make a bad decision. We can all remember, or at least imagine, the thoughts that plague people when they have been touched by evil. People must remember that just because they have been touched by evil, this does not mean that they are *always* going to be vulnerable to evil. They have to get back to trusting again, claiming God's promises in Scripture passages such as Psalm 91, which describe God's protective powers.

Many people's minds are fertile ground for worry. They focus inwardly and are usually concerned about something they cannot control. They can miss the moments at hand in favor of dwelling on the nonsense their minds dig up. The tendency of the mind to dwell on negative ideas is a phenomenon that is far too prevalent. Why doesn't the mind naturally focus on and dwell upon good and positive outcomes? Is it possible to change the pattern or learn to deal with it? In answer to this question, many Christian pastors and teachers would say that there has been a door opened in people's minds through which Satan's ideas enter. This can be the result of sin, guilt, or shame; an issue within the family lineage; a wrong belief; or even mental illness. Each of these can be dealt with.

If you are living in sin, stop today. Confess, change your ways, and accept God's forgiveness. If the sin happens again, remember that the blood of Christ continually cleanses you of all unrighteousness, as we read in 1 John 1:9. If you feel guilt or shame, then you need to surrender those feelings to the Lord and accept God's unconditional love. Thoughts that God imparts are not associated with condemnation but, rather, gentle encouragement to do the next right thing. Satan loves to dig up sins from your past and beat you over the head with them. Many struggle with condemnation and confusion over these reminders, but they need not be issues once they are covered by the blood of Christ through confession, repentance, and faith.

Generate selective amnesia and forget the bad things in favor of

Biblical Principles for Successful Living

moving forward, casting your cares onto God. Look forward to the next opportunity to do right. Christ has forgiven you. A lack of forgiveness of yourself or others is a bad thing that must be eliminated. Forgive immediately and move on. Refusing to forgive someone hurts you worse than the person you are refusing to forgive. If you have inherited a negative mental example based upon sin, destructive events, or perhaps parental example, pray against it and cast it out by the authority of Jesus Christ. It does not need to be repeated in your life.

Remember the secret of your thoughts: You cannot think about two things at once. Stay busy and fill your mind and life with good people, interesting or useful tasks to accomplish, and, most importantly, the Word of God. Jeremiah 17:7 says, "Blessed is the man who trusts in the LORD, and whose hope is the LORD." Blessed indeed!

Another verse, Isaiah 26:3, states that God will keep in perfect peace those whose minds are stayed on Him. Learn to really trust God in all things. Give it all to Him and fear not. When you are tormented, consider it a good training ground and count it all joy that your faith, more precious than gold, is being tried and tested — and will one day give glory to God. Use the bad times to learn and grow. And remember that you are commanded not to fear!

A football quarterback who throws an interception, or a place kicker who misses a critical field goal, has to forget it totally in order to focus properly on the next opportunity. Forget what lies behind, even a few minutes ago, and look forward in faith to living in peace in the present moment and accomplishing what God has for you. To live in victory, you should immediately forget your failures as they occur, never looking back, always looking forward in faith, expecting a God result. Believe that God sees you in a favorable light — because, in Christ, HE DOES.

Chapter 19
Satan's Dilemma — Then and Now

Long ago, on a hill far away — unless you live in Israel — the world was changed forever. The Son of God was crucified, killed, buried, and raised from the dead. In His death, burial, and resurrection, He conquered death, hell, and the grave. The Son of God was made manifest to destroy the works of the devil (see 1 John 3:8), and He succeeded, enabling man's forgiveness and personal reconciliation to God, as well as healing and eternal life.

Ironically, the devil is the one who inspired people to crucify and kill Jesus. The devil apparently thought that killing the Son of God would ensure that He would not save the world. However, Jesus' death, burial, and resurrection ensured Satan's demise and provided the way of salvation to the whole world.

Satan's problem is no different now than it was some two thousand years ago. Every day, Satan comes against believers, using his only weapon, the harassment of believers, seeking to destroy them. He thinks that the pain and destruction or mental turmoil he causes will stop believers from being effective. Through direct and indirect activities, he seeks to rob, kill, and destroy believers. Often, he succeeds — in the short term. This is the same tactic he used with Jesus.

However, just as Jesus overcame Satan while being tempted in the desert and at the cross, each believer can take the fiery darts that Satan fires at them and decide to let those darts make them stronger and more determined to prevail. With each trial and tribulation, the believer can choose to make his or her own faith stronger and continue on as an even more determined foe of the evil one. If you let Him, God will take every negative event in life through which you are required to trust Him, and He will temper your faith like steel. This happens as you learn from experience that He really is faithful every time.

If you were raised in poverty, this may inspire you to achieve financial independence. If your family situation was not ideal, this may inspire you to become a great parent and faithful spouse. If you were bullied as a youngster and survived the bullying, it may cause you to want to help people. These motivations may spring from undesirable events, but they often do lead to desirable results.

Satan does not have power over you or over how you will react, but in this life, there will be trouble. When trouble comes, use it to make yourself stronger, recognizing the battle that we are all engaged in. In so doing, you will, as Jesus did, end up furthering the Kingdom of God with every trial and tribulation you face. The unpleasant issues of life and the weaknesses that plague you are most often viewed as liabilities. In reality, they can be assets, inspiring you to develop, overcome, and excel.

Chapter 20

Stay on the Path

In your diligence to pursue God, avoid spiritual "bunny trails," such as too much emphasis on spiritual warfare, prophecy, doctrine, or personal behavior. Stay mainstream most of the time — resting in what Jesus has already accomplished and appropriating it by faith. Stay focused on the grace and love of God in your life to the point where it transforms your behavior naturally. Let faith work through love so that you are predominantly outwardly focused. The most important tenet of the faith and, indeed, the most important doctrine of the Christian church is "salvation by grace alone through faith alone in Christ alone." Let your faith, working through love, lead you to serving others.

The Bible tells us that Jesus is the Savior of the world. In Deuteronomy 18 He is also revealed as the Prophet who was to come, who will tell us how to obey God. No one can know God except by His revelation through the Holy Spirit. It is possible to know the Bible but not the author, so beware and check yourself often. We cannot fool God. That is why the question "Does salvation by grace mean that I can believe in God and live any way that I want to?" is a silly question. This would not be the question of a sincere Christ-follower who really understands the gift he or she has received. If you approach Him with a sincere heart, searching for Him, He will be your constant guide and get you through the dangerous pathways where many go astray.

The Christian life must be guided by the Holy Spirit, who comes to live in us when we sincerely believe in Christ as Savior. He keeps us "between the ditches." There are distractions on each side of the narrow road to eternal life. Only God can keep us on the road to salvation.

William Lake

Only the sacrifice of His Son, and our sincere faith in Him, will do the transaction. We owe it all to God, and we must never forget that. The Bible teaches eternal security for the truly saved. But we should do our due diligence to check ourselves and ensure we are on track at all times.

Most religious systems try every possible way to eliminate the risk of eternal damnation, seeking to control eternal destiny via behavior modification and sacrifice. The harder the religious system, the more likely it is that we will be going to heaven if we follow it — right? In truth, only humble trust and the willing receipt of the free gift of God can secure our journey heavenward. God's kind gift of grace, through God-given faith, is all we have to count on — be sure you never forget that. That is the narrow road. You stay on the road by trusting and loving God — no matter what. You stay on the road by abiding in His love.

Are you following all of God's precepts as best you know them? I recommend that totally, because your desire to do so is a good sign of true conversion. Despite what some teach these days, there is no error of theology in obeying everything that God has given us to follow that might apply to us now from the Old Testament as well as the New. And, of course, Jesus Christ is our example. We are to walk as He walked (1 John 2:6). But be careful to follow Him out of humble and thankful obedience, lest you become proud and self-confident in your religious performance — instead of God-confident. That's the danger.

Does your behavior give you the sense that you have performed well enough to inherit the Kingdom of God? If so, you are nearing a ditch. Obedience can bring peace, but it must never be the source of our assurance. Remember that there are people who have performed the works of God, such as miracles and healings, who may hear Jesus say, "Depart from me, I never knew you," when they meet the Lord at judgment (see Matthew 7:21-23).

On the other hand, do you proudly proclaim that you can live any way that you want to because you are covered by grace? That's a warning sign! That should not be the heart condition of the believer. Do you think you know all the answers and do not need to spend time daily with God? Another danger zone! Do you attend church two or more times per week but lack the all-important characteristic of love for your fellow man, as evidenced by helping others? Another warning sign! Do you see God's hand move and the gifts of the Spirit manifested but rarely take time to thank and praise Him? Are you always primarily seeking to get God to give you more stuff? Learn to love Him!

There are some thought-provoking — and frightening — verses in Hebrews 6. Verses 4-8 say: "For it is impossible for those who were once enlightened, and have tasted the heavenly gift, and have become partakers of the Holy Spirit, and have tasted the good word of God and the powers of the age to come, if they fall away, to renew them again to repentance, since they crucify again for themselves the Son of God, and put Him to an open shame." If you are seeking God and want to know Him, do not let this passage trouble you. I will not go into great depth here, but some maintain that the passage applies to believers, while others think it applies only to those who stop just short of believing. Still others believe this applies to those who stop short of embracing grace in favor of following the Law. But I am certain that, in any case, we should guard our hearts with all diligence to prevent our own apostasy, or walking away — if that is possible.

I have lived a performance-based Christian life so focused on my behavior that I neglected to seek His face and live out His love to others at times. What I have realized from these experiences is that a constant focus on one's self is, without a doubt, the most depressing and energy-consuming practice you can engage in. If you can learn to forget yourself, trust God, and help others, you will get "into the zone." Take a deep breath and forget yourself, putting your eyes squarely on the Savior. Focus on Him and others. Stay busy and keep moving forward. Refuse to meditate on your past or your future. Trust God in your present circumstances.

God's Word says to measure, or evaluate, yourself by the amount of faith God has given you (see Romans 12:3). It also says that three things abide — faith, hope, and love — and the greatest thing is love (1 Corinthians 13:13). Love should be your trademark as a Christian and your principal motivation for every "religious" thing you do. Christian behaviors motivated by the love of God and fellow man will stand through the judgment of the believer and yield great reward.

The more methods of knowing and pleasing God that you attempt, the more you will realize that it is only faith in God that you can truly count on. It has always been by faith. If you have it, be sure to thank Him.

It is the essential gift. What is the narrow way that Jesus speaks of? The narrow way is not more and more effort on your part, but it is abiding in His love as your "daddy." A true loving relationship of trust with the Savior will result in a more peaceful life and an eternity with Him.

The narrow way is actually characterized by resting in God's provision, developing a love relationship with your heavenly Father through Jesus, and abiding in that love, letting Christ live through you.

Chapter 21

Some Scriptures to Think Harder About

1. **John 5:5–6:** "Now a certain man was there who had an infirmity thirty-eight years. ⁶ When Jesus saw him lying there, and knew that he already had been in that condition a long time, He said to him, 'Do you want to be made well?'"

   Do you find it unusual that the Lord would ask a person who had been sick for so many years if he wanted to be well? Of course, since the Lord asked the question, we know it is a great question, but why? Perhaps because the feeling of comfort and the willing acceptance of the miserable situations we may be in are really an excuse for not going further with God. We can get very comfortable in our misery, and we can fear any change. The status quo can also provide us with an excuse for neglecting to try for positive change.

   You really will not be determined to change anything that you are comfortable with and can live with. I have often heard it said that some people "don't feel right if they don't feel wrong." I can empathize completely. People become comfortable with constant self-condemnation. Other people accept their weaknesses in certain areas, using them as convenient excuses for not moving past their current life experiences, opting instead to be comfortable in spiritual or personal mediocrity.

   Many times, people become accustomed to second-best outcomes, contented in the misery or mental fog that has accompanied them for so long. One of the key catalysts for change is that you must truly be fed up with the current situation. Too often, however, the status quo is a convenient crutch that gives us the perfect excuse to avoid trying anymore. The phenomenon of not truly wanting to move forward to become spiritually better is far more common than we realize. Check yourself and see what you are stuck in that really needs to be changed. The Bible promises you a much better option if you are willing.

2. **1 Samuel 30:6:** "Now David was greatly distressed, for the people spoke of stoning him, because the soul of all the people was grieved, every man for his sons and his daughters. But David strengthened himself in the Lord his God."

    Often, when we are discouraged or feeling depressed, we simply stew in our own juices, feeling bad and compounding the misery with negative self-talk. We look around for a word from God to encourage us. The advice David's example provides here is most useful. Rather than sticking his finger in the Bible and hoping for a word from God about the Philistines, David *encouraged himself* in the Lord!

    If a friend came to you with a problem or feeling discouraged, you most likely would offer a plethora of encouraging and hopeful advice, including the all-time — and true — favorites that God loves them unconditionally and will work all things for good. You would tell them that He is always with us and will never leave or forsake us — and that this unpleasant time will surely pass. Chances are you would have all sorts of uplifting advice, or at least words of encouragement. Why not apply this technique to yourself?

    David counseled himself and encouraged himself. If you counsel yourself with the same scripturally-based messages of inspiration and hope that you would willingly share with others, you will benefit just as a friend you ministered to might. The Bible says we as Christians have the Holy Spirit and the Word of God for Him to bring to our mind as we need it. Enthusiastically remind yourself that God loves you and will never leave you. He has not changed His mind toward you, nor will He forsake you in this or any other moment. Encourage yourself in the Lord.

3. **2 Corinthians 12:7:** "And lest I should be exalted above measure by the abundance of the revelations, a thorn in the flesh was given to me, a messenger of Satan to buffet me, lest I be exalted above measure."

Biblical Principles for Successful Living

As Christians, we must remember that our primary goal in life is to become more Christlike and develop in ourselves the character of our Savior. This most often happens through some seemingly unpleasant catalysts. When we face trials — persecutions, wrongful accusations, or a host of things that we just don't understand — our first inclination is often to ask, "Why me?" This has often been my first reaction. "Why me, Lord? Why do these things keep happening?" Then I have realized that I always seek the Lord and pray more in times like that. Most of my personal spiritual growth has occurred when clinging to the Bible in prayer, asking God for his constant protection and blessing.

True success in the Christian life is to grow more Christlike, not merely to be happy. The experiences of life reveal more and more to us about our own true nature. Trusting in God at these times delivers us from the slow and subtle spiritual malaise of carefree, problem-free prosperity and develops an iron-clad faith. Be at least a little thankful for trials and tribulations. As they did with Paul and so many others, they will result in a beautiful finished product — making us more Christlike, humble servants of the living God.

4. **Matthew 15:9:** "And in vain they worship Me, teaching as doctrines the commandments of men."

Be careful to seek out the truth from Scripture. The Bible is true as written, but religious systems have intervened over the years to add to or subtract from true doctrine. For example, in Judaism there are those who adhere only to what is written in the Torah, the first five books of Moses. These are called Karaite Jews. However, some Rabbinic Jews also adhere to the oral Torah, or Talmud, which at times is contradictory and far more extensive.[36] Christ warned His followers not to follow the doctrines of some of these men (Pharisees), who in some cases laid heavy burdens on people too difficult to bear that were beyond those required in the Torah.

Early Jewish converts followed large portions of the Torah,

---

[36] Wikipedia Contributors, "Karaite Judaism," *Wikipedia, The Free Encyclopedia,* https://en.wikipedia.org/wiki/Karaite_Judaism.

primarily since they had no other scriptures, and they accepted Christ as their Messiah. The only scripture they had was "Old Testament" scripture such as Moses and the prophets. Gentile Christian converts were given relatively few requirements. In Acts 15:18–21, Paul points out: "Known to God from eternity are all His works. Therefore I judge that we should not trouble those from among the Gentiles who are turning to God, but that we write to them to abstain from things polluted by idols, from sexual immorality, from things strangled, and from blood. For Moses has had throughout many generations those who preach him in every city, being read in the synagogues every Sabbath."

Paul makes it clear in his writings that the Christian is not required to follow the Mosaic Law unto salvation. However, in Christendom, the church has over the years essentially discouraged or forbidden most of the Torah from the practices of Christianity. The festivals (Passover, Pentecost, and Tabernacles), the dietary laws, the Paleo-Hebrew language, and the Sabbath, to name a few, were all discouraged or eliminated for a variety of reasons. In place of these, however, we have acquired many more traditions of men: Christmas, Easter, Sunday Sabbath, the seat of the church outside of Jerusalem.

The Bible tells us that in the New Covenant, the Law is to be written on our hearts. The Law, of course, is the law of God and is found initially in the Torah. We should not, therefore, be averse to its contents, even though we know our salvation is assured by faith in our Messiah, who forgives all of our sins. **People should not fear or be ashamed of any higher level of obedience, but they should fear putting themselves under bondage to the Law, thinking perfect adherence, were that possible, guarantees salvation.** There is a huge difference.

Many modern-day Christians are at least partially Torah-observant, because the Torah says so much about what God likes and dislikes. They celebrate the festivals to some degree, follow the dietary laws, for health reasons primarily, and observe the Sabbath on Saturday. They essentially follow as much of the Torah as they feel is applicable today. The reason people seem to avoid most of Torah is because it is, in its entirety, impossible to follow to the degree Christ outlined especially, and some aspects do not seem applicable today. But there are many parts that are quite easy to follow, very applicable, and offer us an opportunity to know and do what pleases God.

This must not be done as the means unto salvation, however. That would be a serious — perhaps fatal — mistake. It must be done, rather, from a heart of love toward God. A Christian should accept the mercy and grace of God in Christ and live as much as possible as Christ lived. Remember that Christ followed the Torah but not all Rabbinic Judaism. He summarized the law in two precepts: that we should love the Lord our God with all of our heart, soul, mind, and strength; and that we should love our neighbors as ourselves. In doing so, we fulfill all the Law and the Prophets.

Some feel the New Testament actually begins with the book of Acts because Jesus preached and lived under the Law to the Jews. Other scriptures say that we, as Christians, should walk as He walked (1 John 2). And we know Paul and the Council of Jerusalem put very few requirements on Gentile believers but seem to have left the door open for those who choose to read and obey more of God's law, as he knew God would lead them to do over time. If the Bible does not mention Christmas and Easter, but does mention the eternal celebrations of Passover, Pentecost, and Tabernacles — and their fulfillment in Christ — should we not at least acknowledge these in some way? See, for instance, Leviticus 23.

Even so, let's keep in mind that the Mosaic Covenant was a temporary covenant. A number of its requirements are upheld and restated in the New Testament — for instance, nine of the Ten Commandments. The fourth, which begins with "Remember the Sabbath day" (see Exodus 20:8–11), is the one not repeated in the New Testament — though Jesus and Paul are noted in Scripture as observing the Sabbath, and having a day of rest is highly encouraged for everyone.

Jews who have accepted Christ as the Messiah are called Messianic Jews. They follow Jewish customs and accept Jesus (Yeshua) as their Messiah. Likewise, there are Christians who choose to follow some of the Torah. The challenge for them is in determining which parts of the Torah are applicable now to Christians today. Some may not be.

You can figure this one out for yourself. However, let me reiterate that, according to the New Testament, salvation is by faith alone, through grace alone, in Christ alone. We should walk as He walked. Rewards are merit-based in the Kingdom of Heaven. We are wise to avoid the doctrines of men and do only what the Bible says as much as possible. *Stick to what it says.*

Chapter 22

We Want to Meet the Lord and Hear "Well Done"

2 Corinthians 13:5: "Examine yourselves as to whether you are in the faith. Test yourselves. Do you not know yourselves, that Jesus Christ is in you? — unless indeed you are disqualified."

Let the reader understand that our walk with Christ is a slow and steady process of spiritual growth and love for God. My Christian life started with "fire insurance" — accepting Jesus so that I would not go to hell. Then there was a time when I committed my life to God and decided to obey as much as possible, tying faith to actions. It was there that I became most frustrated by my inability to be sinless.

Then, several years later, I gained an understanding of grace versus typical religious law-following, which was most encouraging. And, regrettably, there have been plenty of mistakes and sins along the way — even as a "mature Christian." Finally, I learned to believe that God really loves me. What I say below are some guidelines I believe to be valid. The reader should not get discouraged if they are not "all the way there" yet. No one is. It is the trend or inclination that counts most.

You can inspect your life to see if you have a real relationship with Jesus before you meet Him on Judgment Day. First, check to see if your major focus and orientation is toward God. Always remember that your eternal destiny is secured by faith — and faith alone; but you should desire to obey the Lord as much as you know how. You should have a heart turned toward God. Your failures may be constant and plentiful, but if your desire to know and serve God is sincere, then that is a very good sign that your salvation experience is real. Are you so overcome by the miracle of salvation by grace through faith that you would give everything to Him if God asked you to?

Second, check to see if you are exhibiting the fruit of the Spirit at least to some degree — love, joy, peace, patience, kindness, goodness, gentleness, faithfulness, self-control. You should feel and show Christ's love to others, either by natural inclination or by an act of the will. You should not primarily be judgmental or critical. Your theology should be one that fosters obedience to God and service to others from a joyful and grateful heart based on the mercy and grace that God has shown you. You should not be hateful, but loving and tolerant toward others, though you can still make solid judgments on sin behaviors based on biblical principles. Do you enjoy reading or hearing the Word and praying for others? How about fellowship? Do you see evidence that the Holy Spirit is influencing you and guiding you?

Salvation is a gift. God says He will never leave you or forsake you. Even if you sin badly and are having grave doubts, you can trust in Him if you have sincerely asked for salvation. If the two previous paragraphs tend to define your desired walk with Christ, you are on solid ground. If they do not, then start now, beginning with fully understanding the fact that God loves you.

I was watching a high-intensity college football game. It was a nail-biter right down to the finish — when a player on one team broke through the line and scored what would surely be the winning touchdown. As he ran off the field, he was surrounded by his teammates. He could hardly make it to the team's bench because of the swarm of happy teammates around him. However, all the way to the sideline, I observed him looking intently over the friendly players escorting him, and sometimes straining to look around them. "What is he looking for?" I wondered. His family wasn't on the sideline. His girlfriend, if he had one, was likely not there either.

He was looking for his coach as he delivered the victory to his team and his school. What meant the most to him was the approval of his coach, who no doubt had walked with him on his entire journey, helping prepare him for that day. When he reached the coach, he was greeted with a friendly grasping of the face mask, a few words, and a brief hug. It was

Biblical Principles for Successful Living

clear that the coach's approval meant everything to this young player. He went to his place on the bench with a smile and no doubt a full heart.

As we go through life as Christians, the Lord promises that He will be with us in the form of our counselor and guide — the Holy Spirit. He will tell us which way to go and will help us avoid the pitfalls and traps of life. He will give us wisdom and guidance and answered prayer so that the plan of God in our lives will be accomplished. We will have comfort in sorrow, a sure purpose, and inner joy.

If we put our trust in Christ and seek His face as best we can, never quitting when we fail — which we often will — not giving up when challenging things happen, but turning them instead into growth opportunities ... if we cling to our God as hard as we can, knowing He is clinging to us even harder ... if we refuse to get discouraged to the point of despair, if we just keep going, knowing victory is assured in Christ ... then, when we run off the field of life, we will run into the arms of our Coach and our Father. We will hear these words: "Well done, my good and faithful servant."

Look for the coach.

Chapter 23

The Most Important Day of My Life

Ephesians 3:14–19: "For this reason I bow my knees to the Father of our Lord Jesus Christ, from whom the whole family in heaven and earth is named, that He would grant you, according to the riches of His glory, to be strengthened with might through His Spirit in the inner man, that Christ may dwell in your hearts through faith; that you, being rooted and grounded in love, may be able to comprehend with all the saints what is the width and length and depth and height — to know the love of Christ which passes knowledge; that you may be filled with all the fullness of God."

One day it finally dawned on me that, despite the mixed messages that we hear all around us, God really loves us. He does not want to send us to hell. He is not looking for reasons to condemn us. Instead He is looking for the reason to accept us. He acts and feels and thinks much like a perfect human father would.

God loves us, and if we accept His gift of love and grace in Jesus Christ, we will be with Him forever. Just give Him a chance. Accept the gift of Christ in faith and believe in the Lord for eternal salvation. Let the love of Christ be revealed to you. Realize and know that He loves you and wants you to be with Him forever. He has even given us the only way for this to occur — by sacrificing His beloved Son for us.

Ephesians 1:3–6: "Blessed be the God and Father of our Lord Jesus Christ, who has blessed us with every spiritual blessing in the heavenly places in Christ, just as He chose us in Him before the foundation of the world, that we should be holy and without blame before Him in love, having predestined us to adoption as sons by Jesus Christ to Himself, according to the good pleasure of His will, to the praise of the glory of His grace, by which He made us accepted in the Beloved."

He chose us before the foundation of the world. That's pretty special. This should inspire you to love God with all of your heart. This is the narrow road. You must know that God loves you and accepts you. It is revealed to you by God Himself. If you do not have that revelation, then ask God for it. He gives it to the sincere seeker. As profound and vigorous and complete was His hatred of sin, as seen in the Old Testament, equally profound is His grace and mercy toward us who have accepted the great gift of Jesus, His Son, sacrificed for us.

God now accepts you as His own son or daughter. Live and love in that great revelation. It will change your life — as it changed mine. Night to day. Death to life. God really loves you. He has made the way. "Walk ye in it" (Isaiah 30:21).

Chapter 24

Go with God

Psalm 1:1–6: "Blessed is the man who walks not in the counsel of the ungodly, nor stands in the path of sinners, nor sits in the seat of the scornful; But his delight is in the law of the Lord, and in His law he meditates day and night. He shall be like a tree planted by the rivers of water that brings forth its fruit in its season, whose leaf also shall not wither; and whatever he does shall prosper. The ungodly are not so but are like the chaff which the wind drives away. Therefore the ungodly shall not stand in the judgment, nor sinners in the congregation of the righteous. For the Lord knows the way of the righteous, but the way of the ungodly shall perish."

John learned much on his journey of personal Christian growth, primarily through trial and error over the years of his life. His life was generally more productive and his mental attitude had improved greatly. He routinely employed his daily disciplines such as a morning quiet time and lots of prayer. He always sought to feed his faith. He began to speak with more power and authority — and to use Scripture extensively in his daily routine. He did not meditate on whatever came into his mind but believed what the Word of God said about him. He began to see the hand of God move more and more. Even in the tough times, he just kept going in faith and trust — looking forward to being with his Savior one day. John knew that if he loved God and knew Him as Father, he would never be turned away.

Agree with God early in your life that He has a special purpose for you — and spend time finding out what that purpose is. Obey what God tells you directly through his Word and through His indwelling Holy Spirit. Spend time thinking about, meditating on, and speaking the Word for every situation. Always incorporate healthy doses of praise and thanksgiving. Do not think, speak, or act against God's purpose for you.

God has an enemy — and so do you. Therefore, remember to keep your guard up. Remember that evil and destructive things come from Satan, not from God. Remember that Satan's only real weapons are the thoughts that he puts into our heads. He has no physical presence. He has to work primarily through people, just as God does. Remember that ideas are powerful. Only accept those ideas that pass the test of Scripture and are beneficial to act on. What you believe is most critical.

Put your trust in God and find God's purpose for your life. Then partner with Him to accomplish it. Ask Him frequently for advice and counsel through His indwelling Holy Spirit. Keep yourself free from encumbering distractions, like the many opportunities for sin. Agree with His Word, stay focused, accept forgiveness as often as you need it, and get back up when you are knocked down — every time. Most importantly, rejoice, for the ultimate victory is God's. And that victory is also yours if you choose to stay on the narrow path of salvation by grace alone, through faith alone, in Christ alone — most often evidenced by love, obedience, and gratitude.

Realize that time is short; so believe, speak, and act out only what you want to happen — not that which you do *not* want to happen. Assess every move you plan to make. Will it get you where you want to go? Is it positive, neutral, or detrimental to your God-ordained purpose and your eternity? Do everything you can to kindle a strong, vital faith.

Here are some ideas for fostering strong faith:

1. When you are really aligned with God and you know you are accomplishing His purpose for you, you should not fear failure, because He is responsible for your results. Obey God and leave outcomes to Him. There is no personal agenda when you do exactly what God tells you to do. Frustration comes from dreaming up a purpose on your own and trying to get God to

Biblical Principles for Successful Living

bless it. The things we fear really come from fear of our own personal loss or diminishment.
2. To build faith, focus on the greatness of God. Consider the amazing universe. Realize that whatever you need will be an easy thing for Him. And you know that He wins in the end. One preacher said it's like watching a game and already knowing the result because you recorded it. You really don't have to worry when things look bad. God — and you — will win.
3. Make sure you understand and believe that you are the righteousness of God in Christ. When you know this fact deep in your heart, the devil cannot convict you of sin any longer and cannot cause you to feel condemned for your past, present, or future sin. If you are a true believer, then your errant behavior does not affect your standing with God or make Him love you less.
4. Be sure to obey what God and the laws of the land say. Obedience keeps you largely free from fear, condemnation, and the attacks of Satan. It will help you become full of faith.
5. God is no respecter of persons, so remember that what He has done for one person, He will do for another. You can do anything He wants you to do according to His Word.
6. Be expectant. Believe in God's ability and willingness to help you meet your purpose and need. He has ordained you from the beginning of time to accomplish certain things.
7. Spend a lot of time reading the Word and in prayer. The more Word you learn in your heart by revelation through meditation, the stronger your faith becomes. It is hard to have a powerful faith if you do not spend time in the Word or in fellowship with God daily.
8. Most importantly, tie your life's purpose and your efforts and resources to the Kingdom of God, and He will bless and protect them.
9. Meditate on the fact that *God really loves you unconditionally.*

Remember to continue to learn how to hear from God. He speaks in a still small voice. Satan will "loudly" offer guilt, condemnation, fear, anger, and hatred. He will put you into turmoil if he can. He will drain your energy and distract you. God will offer wisdom. If He is suggesting something, He will normally do it very gently. What God suggests may sound silly to you or may not make sense. This may well be a sign that it is from God, in that it is not what you personally think or want. Psalm 37:4 says that He will put His desires in our hearts if we delight ourselves in Him.

In life, most people do not believe big. So, shoot for the stars and dream big. Never limit yourself. Do not run a race looking backwards — and don't drive down the highway of life looking into the rear-view mirror. Forget the past. Similarly, you should not ignore God if you want to live a fulfilling life and to be with Him forever. Why don't you do the things that will get you to the place you want to go? Why work against yourself by saying and doing destructive things?

One of my favorite verses is Ecclesiastes 9:4: *"But for him who is joined to all the living there is hope, for a living dog is better than a dead lion."* Live large and don't be in a rush to die. It will come quickly enough when God is done with you here.

Do not agree with the devil about any limiting idea. Take all the limits off of God and your dreams. Watch out for any thought you have which causes you to question what God says. "Has God really said that?" Those were substantially the devil's words to Eve in the garden (see Genesis 3:1). Satan is the great deceiver. Guard your mind because you will probably do what you are thinking about the most. Monitor and adjust your self-talk because, for many, it tends to be negative.

Search for all the agreements you have made with the devil as a result of suggestions or advice or experiences during your lifetime and stop them cold. Do not let the devil tell you that you will never be good at certain school subjects, certain sports, or anything else. Just do the work to become good at what you really want. Do not let Satan tell you that you are too sinful to be saved and go to heaven. Do not let him tell you that your life does not count for God. Do not let him tell you it's too late. Do not let him tell you that your sin will separate you from God once you are born again. Guard your mind and remove limiting and debilitating thoughts from it.

Your salvation is a free gift. Accept it gladly and permanently. Live a life of obedience and generosity from a heart of love and thanksgiving. Do good for everyone you can at all times. Be generous and inspirational to others and enjoy your life. No matter what happens, it is very unlikely that being negative or critical will make it better, so stay positive. God never promised you a bed of roses, but He did promise you eternal life in Christ Jesus and that He would always be with you.

You're going to have to actually do something with what you read in this book. You cannot just read it and forget it and go on to the next thing. If you don't act on it and make the necessary adjustments, then there will be no change for the better in your situation. Assess your life at the time you read this book. If you are pleased with its direction and quality, that is good. That means you are headed where you want to go and that your daily routines are aligned accordingly. If you are not pleased with the direction in which you are headed, the manner in which things happen for you, or what you have achieved, then it's time to make changes in your habits and routines.

The first thing will be to ask the Lord for the vision for your life. Once you have that vision, you should take steps to achieve it. If you can do it yourself, then do it. If you need to form a team, form a team. Seek mentors who have achieved what you are seeking to achieve. Think thoughts and take actions which move you closer to your goals each day. Ensure that your thoughts, words, and habits are aligned with your purpose. And never, ever quit.

Don't allow sin, or discouragement, or disappointment to distract you. Keep focused on your purpose. Don't be overly self-centered, and don't stay angry or offended. Paul counsels us in Ephesians 4:26: "Do not let the sun go down on your wrath." If you can learn to see the greater good in the fulfillment of God's kingdom purposes, instead of simply your own interests, you are on the right path. If you can release anger through forgiveness, and humbly realize your own relative importance in the world, then you will be successful.

Learn to take God at his word and avoid learning only from all of your own mistakes. Whenever possible, learn from the mistakes of others. He who will accept instruction will generally be more successful in life. He who will not heed instruction is bound for failure. Before major decisions, seek the counsel of at least three godly people you respect and who know you, your situation, and the Word. Proverbs 11:14 says there is safety in a multitude of counselors.

With all great visions, dreams, or plans, be willing to take things slowly. God directs us not to despise the time of small beginnings (see Zechariah 4:10). Very few worthwhile things ever went from nothing to something great in a very short time. And most great people were also failures at some point. That's how they learned. The real secret is that they never quit. You can learn many of their lessons through books.

This great life drama that you are in is not about you. It's about God and His plan. The best thing you can do for yourself and your family is to fit into God's grand plan. Go where He is and do what He tells you to do. Don't just do whatever you conceive of and ask God to bless it. When you make a mistake, get back up and try again, knowing that grace covers you. Don't be bound by past mistakes, but rather be your own best friend. Forgive yourself, as God has forgiven you and as you forgive others, and move on.

A close relationship with God takes effort. Romans 10:17 tells us, "Faith comes by hearing and hearing by the Word of God." Strong faith takes work and the study of and meditation on the Word. You cannot ignore God and expect to have a strong faith. You have to spend time with God daily for strong faith, salvation, healing, well-being, freedom from oppression, and all of God's blessings. Remember that He rewards faith above all. Without faith, as Hebrews 11:6 counsels us, it is impossible to please God.

If you apply the principles discussed herein, then you will greatly increase your chances for a meaningful, successful life; more importantly, a good legacy; and, most importantly, a successful eternity.

> **Proverbs 23:22–25:** "Listen to your father who begot you, and do not despise your mother when she is old. Buy the truth, and do not sell it, also wisdom and instruction and understanding. The father of the righteous will greatly rejoice, and he who begets a wise child will delight in him. Let your father and your mother be glad, and let her who bore you rejoice."

Biblical Principles for Successful Living

> **Ecclesiastes 7:8:** "The end of a thing is better than its beginning."

It's not how you start; it's how you finish. So, finish strong!

One last point: If you are not a Christian and would like to become one, you must **believe in the Lord Jesus Christ**.

Say the following prayer to God in faith:

> **Dear Heavenly Father, I am a sinner and I need to be saved by Your grace. I put my trust in You and Your Son, Jesus Christ, and ask You to forgive me for all I have done and all I may yet do. Please save my soul, accept me as your child, and make me the person you want me to be. Thank you for saving my soul today. In Jesus' name, AMEN!**

Now, be sure to immediately seek to attend a Bible-believing church to get mentored by seasoned believers. Let the Spirit of God lead you into a rich and fulfilling life as a Christian child of Almighty God by the grace He has shown you in giving His Son as a sacrifice for your sins, and by raising Him from the dead to give you eternal life.

> **John 15:9:** "As the Father loved Me, I also have loved you; abide in My love."

Printed in the United States
By Bookmasters